C000260211

The Spokesman
The Narrative of Peace
Edited by Tony Simpson

Published by Spokesman for the
Bertrand Russell Peace Foundation
Ken Coates: Editor 1970 to 2010

Spokesman 118   2012

K)

CONTENTS

Thanks to Steve Bell

*Cover: Iroji Kebeni, a Marshallese boy, suffered radiation burns to his
skin after contact with 'Bikini snow' – radioactive ash and coral
fragments dispersed over the Marshall Islands from US nuclear testing
at Bikini Atoll in the Pacific Ocean during the 1940s and 1950s.*

Back issues available
on request

A CIP catalogue record
for this book is available
from the British Library

Published by the
Bertrand Russell Peace
Foundation Ltd.,
Russell House
Bulwell Lane
Nottingham NG6 0BT
England
Tel. 0115 9784504
email:
elfeuro@compuserve.com
www.spokesmanbooks.com
www.russfound.org

FSC

Mixed Sources
Product group from well-managed
forests and other controlled sources

Cert no. SGS-COC-006541
www.fsc.org
© 1996 Forest Stewardship Council

ISSN 1367 7748   Printed by the Russell Press Ltd., Nottingham, UK   ISBN 978 0 85124 820 2

DUCCKALAUREATE SHiT PART 2:

belltoons.co.uk

-©Steve Bell 2012 - 3387 · 18·9·12-

Editorial

Coalition Politics

Nick Clegg's YouTube hit 'I'm Sorry' is but one song in a festival of *mea culpas* from the deputy prime minister, as the sustained attempt to resuscitate his political fortunes founders against the growing economic and political crisis which now afflicts Britain. His broken promises on student fees are compounded by disappearing courses, as the market in higher education renders some of them, and their teachers, 'uneconomic'. Direct public funding for humanities courses has ceased altogether. Undergraduates commencing university courses in 2012 face an accumulated bill on completion in excess of £50,000. The common advice to such students is to borrow as much as possible, as they're unlikely to earn enough to pay it all back during the 30 years following graduation. On current reckoning, graduates would need a starting salary of about £38,000 to be on course to complete the repayments. Some chance!

But, while Mr Clegg seemingly self-flagellates, he and David Cameron have handed another Lib Dem a get-out-of-jail card by making David Laws the new Minister of State for Schools and the Cabinet Office, where he has a 'cross-department role working on the Coalition Agreement and government policy'. Among other things, the MP for Yeovil (Paddy Ashdown's old turf) is charged with driving through the abolition of national pay agreements for teachers and other staff while advancing conversion of their schools to independent academies so that they no longer are part of the local authority. How is it that his rehabilitation has been so rapid?

In April 2011, the Parliamentary Commissioner for Standards found that, over a number of years since his election in 2001, Mr Laws had claimed substantial Parliamentary allowances to which he was not entitled (see below). Once caught, Mr Laws quickly repaid more than £56,000. No shortage of cash there. Although the sum was considerable, the calculated deceptions and errors of judgement revealed in the Commissioner's 284-page report are all the more worrying, given the Minister's new responsibilities for schools.

Apparently, Mr Laws remains popular in the City of London where, according to recent press reports, he was paid £5,000 for four hours' work, before Mr Cameron's phonecall. As Ken Coates informed us in *Spokesman 109*, Laws had been a banker, first as Vice President at J P Morgan and Company, and then Managing Director of Barclays De Zoete Wedd, before becoming Director of Policy for the Liberal Democrats between 1997 and

1999. Once elected to Parliament, in 2001, he edited *The Orange Book,* published in 2004 to reclaim Liberalism for the 'free market', and away from the clutches of Charles Kennedy, the Lib Dem leader who had dared to oppose the Iraq War *before* it was started.

Here is Laws' great merit in the eyes of the Cameron/Clegg Coalition. He, like them, is a neo-liberal, ideologically opposed to public provision. That is why one of the first acts of the Coalition Government was to legislate for the widespread establishment of those publicly funded independent schools known as academies. Formerly, most of these had been part of the local authority. At a stroke, billions of pounds worth of public assets passed into the ownership of new charitable companies limited by guarantee. Some were absorbed into academy chains of several schools. There's much money to be made in education these days, as Mr Laws and Michael Gove know very well. For they seem to share a key aspect of Orange Book Liberalism

'which is the belief in the value of free trade, open competition, market mechanisms, consumer power, and the effectiveness of the private sector. These beliefs are combined with opposition to monopolies and instinctive suspicion of State control and interference particularly in relationship to the ownership and control of business.'

So it is that falsifying expenses to the tune of tens of thousands of pounds should not be a bar to high office, even before the electorate has had a chance to pass its own judgement on such conduct,

Tony Simpson

*   *   *

Excerpts from the Memorandum of the
Parliamentary Commissioner for Standards

Rt Hon David Laws

i. Mr Laws wrongly designated as his main home his Somerset property in his constituency from April 2005, since, by then, he was spending substantially more nights in his London accommodation than in his Somerset property… It follows that all his second home claims after April 2005 were made on the wrong property.

ii. Mr Laws' conduct in the submission of his tenancy agreements was not above reproach, because he submitted misleading agreements to the Fees Office from 2001 to 2008 with the result that the Fees Office had no opportunity to challenge or advise him about the propriety of his claims against the Green Book rules. This was in breach of the injunction that claims should be above reproach in successive editions of the Green Book ...

iii. Mr Laws was in breach of the rules of the House from July 2006 to July 2009 in claiming for the costs of leasing accommodation from the person with whom he shared each of the two properties in London over that time, since that person was his partner under the terms of the prohibition on leasing such accommodation from a partner in section 3.3.3 of the 2006 Green Book: they were living together and treated each other as spouses. It follows that all Mr Laws' claims arising from his lease of that accommodation from his partner over that period were in breach of that rule.

iv. Mr Laws was in breach of the rules of the House in the claims he made for rent in staying in these two properties from at least 2004 (the earliest year for which figures are available) to July 2009 since the monthly rental claims were substantially more than the costs which could be justified as having been wholly, exclusively and necessarily incurred while living with his landlord in these properties ... The result was that his rental claims benefited someone close to him, namely his partner who owned the properties and who lived with him in them ...

v. Mr Laws was in breach of the rules of the House in claiming for repairs and maintenance work undertaken on the second London home in 2007–08, since these additional expenses were not necessarily incurred by him given that his rental claims were already significantly above that which could be justified by his share of living in the property in a sound condition, with the result that his claims for building work benefited someone close to him, namely his partner who owned the property and who lived in it with him ...

vi. Mr Laws was in breach of the rules of the House from 2001 to March 2009 in the claims he made for his telecommunications costs which covered his main home in his constituency and his mobile phone as well as his calls from his London homes ...

I consider that Mr Laws' breaches of the rules in respect of his second home claims were serious. I have no evidence that Mr Laws made his claims with the intention of benefiting himself or his partner in conscious breach of the rules. But the sums of money involved were substantial. He made a series of breaches. Some of them continued over a number of years ...

John Lyon CB
28 April 2011

Our foremost socialist dramatist

Trevor Griffiths is a friend and comrade of the Russell Foundation of many years, going back to the 1960s and visits to London's Red Café. In 1978, he served on the jury of the Third Russell Tribunal, which examined *Berufsverbote*, or bans on employment in the public service on political grounds and related aspects of human rights in what was then West Germany. Ten years ago, in 2002, he travelled to Cordoba in Spain to participate in a dialogue on peace and human rights which brought together activists from Europe, the Middle East and more widely. The threat of coming war in Iraq hung over the assembly, which argued strongly and cogently for a 'Middle East zone free of weapons of mass destruction, nuclear, chemical and biological'.

All the time, Griffiths was writing, adding to a distinguished and substantial body of work for the theatre, film and television. In 1982, Spokesman published *Sons and Lovers*, his sparkling screenplay for the BBC's memorable adaptation of Lawrence's coalfield novel. Twenty years on, in 2002, prior to Cordoba, we commenced publishing in *The Spokesman* an occasional series of Griffiths's texts. The first was *Camel Station*, a short play with a very good joke, set in Iraq's Northern No-Fly Zone (*Spokesman 75*).

In 2005, at Ken Coates's instigation, Spokesman published Griffiths's full-length screenplay about Thomas Paine, *These Are the Times*. Kurt Vonnegut loved it so much he declared that he wished he had written it, and requested dozens of copies to send to friends in Hollywood, some of whom did indeed promise to try to get the film made. A short excerpt was published in *Spokesman 91*. Subsequently, the work was adapted for the stage, under the title *A New World,* and premiered at The Globe in London to wide acclaim in 2009. A BBC radio adaptation, with Jonathan Pryce as Paine, brought the work to new ears.

Meanwhile, Griffiths had entrusted Spokesman with publishing his collected *Theatre Plays* in two volumes, which appeared in 2007. Fifteen plays, written and performed during more than 40 years, included classics such as *The Party*, *Comedians*, and Griffiths's scintillating version of Chekhov's *The Cherry Orchard* (premiered at Nottingham Playhouse in March 1997, directed by Richard Eyre, when the audience spontaneously applauded the opening set), as well as *The Gulf between Us*, which grew out of the first Gulf War in 1991, and *Thatcher's Children*, first performed at Bristol Old Vic in 1993.

Michael Billington, *The Guardian's* redoubtable and humane theatre critic, remarked that 'Trevor Griffiths is the godfather of British political theatre' and rightly described him as 'our foremost socialist dramatist'. Billington went on to urge a new production of *Occupations*, Griffiths's first full-length play for the stage about factory occupations in northern Italy in 1920, which received its first production at the Stables Theatre in Manchester in 1970. Now that would be a timely revival!

In 2008, the screenplay for *Willie and Maud* (W B Yeats and Maude Gonne) was first published in *Spokesman 98*, followed in early 2012 by *Habbacuc Dreams*. As part of the 400th anniversary celebrations of the publication of the King James Bible, the Bush Theatre in London had invited contemporary 'responses' to the 66 books of the Bible. In between, in 2009, we published Ann Talbot's extended review of *A New World* at The Globe, together with songs from the play.

Now, we are pleased to fulfil a longstanding commitment made by Ken Coates to Trevor Griffiths that *The Spokesman* would publish *March Time*, his screenplay homage to the Labour Movement down the ages. Originally written in 1987, in the midst of Thatcherism, and revised in 1994, as Tony Blair stole the Labour Party, *March Time* has been revised again for publication here. As neo-liberal destruction of public provision reaches deep into education and the health service, and 'austerity' is seen to be not for the rich but only for the rest of us 'plebs', it couldn't be more fitting.

Tony Simpson

JOHN GITTINGS

THE *Glorious* ART *of* PEACE

From the
Iliad to Iraq

The Narrative of Peace

What we can learn from the history of thinking about peace

John Gittings

John Gittings was for many years chief foreign leader-writer and East Asia Editor at The Guardian. *His new book,* The Glorious Art of Peace: From the Iliad to Iraq, *is published by Oxford University Press. It will be reviewed in our next issue.*

War still has a much higher visibility than peace, in spite of the flourishing of peace studies over the last three to four decades, and many people are unaware that there is a science of peace which is every bit as complex and rich as the science of war. A survey of the shelves of any large bookshop or library will illustrate the point: it is much easier to find Sunzi on the *Art of War* than the thoughts on peace of his Chinese contemporary Mengzi. Machiavelli's militaristic counsel to *The Prince* is much more accessible than the pacific advice to another Prince of his Renaissance contemporary Erasmus. Clausewitz's thoughts *On War* are more likely to be on the shelves than the reflections *On Perpetual Peace* by his fellow thinker of the Enlightenment, Immanuel Kant. And for a round-up of thinking on peace and war, while the Oxford reader on *War* (Freedman, ed., 1994) is generally available, the Oxford reader on *Approaches to Peace* (Barash, ed., 2000), is much less so. Yet, over the last two millennia, there has been a powerful and multi-stranded narrative of peace, expressed in different forms and in different environments, challenging the more familiar dialogue of war. This trajectory of pacific thought is not just of scholarly interest but can still enrich our contemporary debate on how to fashion a more peaceful world. Here I shall trace it (briefly and selectively) from ancient China and Greece, through early Christian thought to the humanist thinkers of the Renaissance, onwards in an increasingly rich dialogue through the Enlightenment into the 19th century when peace became a campaigning issue and the modern peace movement can be said to have emerged. I shall then consider what lessons we can draw from this still under-explored wealth of peace thinking which may continue to be relevant today.

I
The History of Peace Thought

The Ancient World

Our journey begins in China during the 4th-3rd century BC – the period of the Warring States which led to the first unification of China (221BC) – when we may listen in on a vigorous debate between scholar-advisers of the different Schools of thought (the so-called Hundred Schools) on the merits of peace and war. The 'Legalists' valued military force above all else and claimed that aggression was the best form of defence. The Strategists provided the city-state rulers with strategic and tactical advice, most famously in Sunzi's *Art of War,* which is still studied by military commanders to this day. Powerful arguments in favour of peace were also made at the court by Confucian and Mohist scholars, though these are less familiar to us today. War is almost always a disaster, they told their rulers, and it inflicts grievous harm on the ordinary people who bear its brunt. In the words of the Confucian scholar Mengzi (Mencius):

> *In wars to win land, the dead fill the fields; in wars to seize cities, the dead fill their streets. This is what we mean by 'teaching the earth how to eat human flesh'.*

The king should rule with humanity and justice, not by fear and terror, they advised, and if properly treated, then his people will rally to resist aggression. Good government is not only moral but the best form of defence. Mozi, founder of the Mohist school, went further, suggesting that the obligation extended beyond state boundaries. One has a duty to help a potential enemy whose people are suffering from starvation or drought rather than take advantage of his weakness. In this way the ruler can break the cycle of violence by performing 'an act of unilateral benefit'. The Daoists (Taoists) also contributed to the peace debate. Contrary to the general view today, their legendary founder Laozi did not reject the world or advocate withdrawing from it altogether. His advice rather was to conform with what was spontaneous and harmonious – and therefore peaceful – in life.

> *Let the people live a simple life, enjoy their food and find beauty in their clothes, be happy where they live and be content in their abode. Though the peoples of neighbouring states live so close that they can hear their neighbours' chickens squawk and the dogs bark, yet they can grow old side by side while leaving each other alone. (Daodejing, ch. 80)*

Our perception of classical Greece in the city-state era (5th to 4th centuries BC) is also dominated by war, although there were constant efforts, sometimes resulting in success, to maintain peace through treaties and diplomacy. The history of this period has been biased by the war-oriented approach of Thucydides who, in his *History of the Peloponnesian War*, presents at length the arguments of the war party in the Athenian Assembly, but barely mentions those who urged peace. Thus, the speech by Pericles advocating war with Sparta (432 BC) is given in full, while the argument of those urging compromise is summarised in half a sentence. Later, in describing the peace concluded in 422 BC (the Peace of Nicias), Thucydides barely mentions war weariness as a factor. We must rely on Plutarch's much later life of the Athenian leader Nicias for a rare glimpse (in a passage based on a source no longer available to us) of the strong desire for peace among the Athenians.

> *They really did regard the peace as the work of Nicias, just as they considered the war the work of [the belligerent Athenian leader] Pericles. The one was held to have involved the Greeks in calamitous disasters, for no very good reason, while the other managed to persuade them to forget all their terrible injuries and become friends.*

Early Christianity and Peace

The early Christian fathers thought deeply about peace, raising questions – still relevant today – about the real meaning of the injunctions of Jesus Christ, and the balance to be struck between temporal and spiritual obligations. Christians in the imperial service of Rome faced a hard choice between unquestioning obedience and conscientious objection. The message of the early fathers, such as Origen and Tertullian, was that Christianity (in the phrase of Justin Martyr) had 'changed the instruments of war, the swords into ploughs and the spears into farming implements'. This record of early Christian pacifism has been played down and sometimes ignored altogether in some standard histories of the origins of Christianity. One of the most striking stories from this period is that of Martin (b. AD 316), the young Roman soldier who told his emperor that he would henceforth refuse to fight and become a solder of Christ instead. Even after the historic compromise between the church and the Emperor, this story shows, there were Christians who continued to believe that military service was incompatible with their faith. The tale of Martin could be described as one of the first recorded cases of conscientious objection. All the more amazing therefore, that in an ironic reversal of roles, St Martin of Tours has become in the Catholic faith the patron saint of soldiers!

The role of St Augustine (AD 354-430) has been subjected to similar distortion: in many accounts, his greatest contribution was to resolve the dilemma faced by early Christians between their temporal and spiritual obligations by formulating the doctrine of the Just War, of which he is said to be the 'father'. Yet nowhere in Augustine's abundant writings is this doctrine spelt out clearly, and he would not approve of the use which has been made of his words to justify numerous wars. In his great work, *The City of God,* Augustine was far more eloquent on the subject of peace. In the city of man as well as in Heaven, he wrote, there is a desire for peace which may be achieved on earth to some degree. Even the warrior who had to take up arms, said Augustine, should regard 'the prevention of shedding blood as his real mission'. Man's nature moves him powerfully 'to maintain peace with all other men as far as he is able', and anyone who can contemplate warfare without heartfelt grief has 'lost all human feeling'.

The Crusades is another episode in history where the voices of the warriors and those who support them sound loud and clear down the ages, while the voices of those opposed to such adventures are heard dimly if at all. Opposition within sections of the Church and nobility, and in the emerging urban societies, can usually only be discerned through the counter-arguments deployed by advocates of the Crusades. The clearest evidence for opposition in the late thirteenth century comes in the memorandum of Humbert of Romans, the senior Dominican who sought to demolish the arguments of the critics. Humbert cited in detail eight 'hindrances' to the crusade, and seven types of men who objected to it foremost were those who believed that the Crusades were not compatible with Christianity.

Peace Thought in the Renaissance

The modern debate on peace and war may be said to have begun in the Renaissance, with the arguments of two great scholars in the humanist tradition, Niccolò Machiavelli (1469-1527) and Desiderius Erasmus (1466-1536), occupying opposite poles. The contrast may be illustrated by these two pieces of advice, both taken from essays intended to instruct a prince on how to conduct himself as a ruler.

Erasmus:

> *The first and most important objective is the instruction of the Prince in the matter of ruling wisely during times of peace, in which he should strive his utmost to preclude any future need for the science of war. (Education of a Christian Prince,* 1516)

Machiavelli:

> *A Prince ought to have no other aim or thought, nor select anything else for his study, than war and its rules and discipline; for this is the sole art that belongs to him who rules. (The Prince, 1513)*

Though the two scholars were contemporaneous there is no record that they actually met. However, they were both in Florence at the same time and witnessed a significant military event in neighbouring Bologna from which they drew opposite conclusions – the siege of the city in 1506 by the army of the warlike Pope Julius II (known as Julius the Terrible). For Erasmus this demonstrated the negation of everything that kings and popes should stand for: was Pope Julius the successor of Jesus Christ, he asked, or of Julius Caesar? Later he would write a satirical dialogue in which the Pope, drunk and boasting of his military victories, is denied entry to Heaven by St Peter! Machiavelli on the other hand admired the Pope's firmness of purpose in pursuing his campaign and his refusal to be bound by peace treaties which had been made between previous Popes and the city of Bologna. Later, Machiavelli would praise qualities of this ruthless kind in *The Prince.*

Erasmus was the most eloquent, as well as the most prolific, of a group of Renaissance humanists who, in the early sixteenth century, sought to convince the rulers of the emerging European nation-state system that the interests of potentate and populace alike were best served by peace, not war, and who for a short while believed that their arguments might prevail. Erasmus was in his time much better known than Machiavelli, and his books were widely circulated (Henry VIII possessed his own copy of the *Education of a Christian Prince*). His writings on the subject of peace would, if collected together, occupy some 400 pages of a modern book. Yet we will search today to find these works. Usually, the only available title is his *In Praise of Folly* (1510), a *jeu d'esprit* written for the amusement of fellow-humanist Sir Thomas More – the only work by Erasmus to have been published in the *Penguin Classics* series. This may be contrasted with the ready availability of many of Machiavelli's works. The catalogue of the well-stocked Oxfordshire library service lists 16 editions of works by Machiavelli, and only two by Erasmus.

Peace Thought in the Enlightenment

Free-minded thinkers in the age of Enlightenment identified clearly the threat posed by shifting alliances of nations led by wilful rulers who resorted to war without regard for the suffering it caused. Their thinking was linked by a loose but coherent thread, referring back to earlier advocacy from Erasmus (whose works enjoyed a revival) onwards. Among their forerunners, the French monk Émeric Crucé (1590–1648) stands out: in the *Nouveau Cynée* he proposed a permanent Council of Ambassadors to resolve disputes between states, to be located in Venice. The Quaker scholar and founder of Pennsylvania, William Penn (1644–1718), in his *Essay Towards the Present and Future Peace of Europe* (1693), set out a more detailed structure for a pan-European council. The French rationalist and early Enlightenment thinker, the Abbé de Saint-Pierre (1658–1743), drew on earlier works for his own *Project for Perpetual Peace* (1712). Jean-Jacques Rousseau (1712–78) would edit Saint-Pierre's *Project*, adding a 'judgement' or commentary of his own. This discourse of peace in the Enlightenment reaches its peak with Immanuel Kant (1724–1804), whose essay on *Perpetual Peace* has received more attention than its predecessors. Kant's plan for a League of Nations (he was the first to use the term), although conceived in a restricted sense, would have a practical influence on the Versailles negotiations a century later.

Kant argued against secret treaties and against the use of mercenaries for the abolition of standing armies and for a republican form of government. Kant's overall vision for perpetual peace is at points difficult to interpret, but he clearly perceives that the maintenance of world peace has to be a joint endeavour, and he identifies the lack of what we would now call 'enforcement' as a major problem. Kant has been accused of advocating an unrealisable utopia but the charge is unfair: he believed that peace is achievable but not inevitable, concluding that it depended in the end on human efforts:

> *In this manner nature guarantees perpetual peace by the mechanism of human passions. Certainly she does not do so with sufficient certainty for us to predict the future in any theoretical sense, but adequately from a practical point of view, making it our duty to work toward this end, which is not just a chimerical one.*

Peace Thought and Action in the 19ᵗʰ Century

The peace societies which began to emerge after the Napoleonic Wars, drawing on a wider social and geographical basis, and driven by the horrors of modern conflict, made it possible for the first time for the voices of tens of thousands rather than of a handful of scholars to be heard on the subject of peace. Although they suffered drastic reversals and were easily silenced by the shrill sound of patriotism whenever a new war broke out, they quickly came back to life when the costs of such a war were reckoned up. By the end of the century they could even lay claim to the support – however equivocal – of a Russian tsar and a multitude of European government ministers. It is easy to dismiss the nineteenth century peace movement for placing too much faith in the power of persuasion and for underestimating the strength of militarism. Yet the First Hague Peace Conference of 1899 did achieve practical results in the fields of arbitration and the regulation of rules of war, while peace and disarmament were placed on the international agenda, where they have remained ever since. The human cost of war, dramatised by a series of senseless conflicts including the Crimean War (1853–6), the Franco-Austrian War (1859) and the Franco-Prussian War (1870–1), also led to first steps towards an international humanitarian law, notably the establishment of the International Committee of the Red Cross.

The movement brought together Christian evangelists, Quakers with a previous history of peace commitment, and secular humanitarians in seeking a more peaceful world. They were driven not only by considerations of morality and compassion, but increasingly by rational arguments as to the harmful socio-economic effects of war and military preparation. By the end of the century, there had emerged a shared vision of a liberal internationalism which saw the need for global organisations which could provide international security without resort to violence. Advocates of peace in the period leading up to World War One include such well-known names as Noah Worcester, Elihu Burritt, Richard Cobden, Victor Hugo, Henry Richard, Bertha von Suttner, Jean de Bloch, Jacques Novikow, John Ruskin, William James, Norman Angell and H G Wells. Today their arguments are mostly either neglected or dismissed as unrealistic, while the thoughts and words of the great writers are glibly dismissed as unrelated to the real genius of their work. Yet the evolution of Tolstoy's thoughts can be traced from his powerful reporting of the Crimean War (which was subjected to Russian censorship), through *War and Peace* when he was still trying to reconcile the apparent inevitability of war with its essential immorality, to the complete rejection of violence and adoption of total pacifism in his later years. Similarly, in the case of Hugo, we can trace a consistent development of his thinking on peace from his address to the first great Peace Conference of 1849 – when he made a prescient appeal for European unity which would make war obsolete – to the impassioned denunciation of war in his speech on the centenary of Voltaire's death (1878) in which he draws a powerful connection between the peace thought of the Enlightenment and the peace campaigns of his own time.

Let us give the word to those great voices [of the Enlightenment]. Let us stop the shedding of human blood. Enough, enough, you despots! If barbarism persists then philosophy must protest. If the sword is relentless, then civilisation must denounce it. Let the 18th century come to the aid of the 19th century! The philosophers who came before us are the apostles of truth, let us invoke the illustrious shadows of those who, faced by monarchs who dreamt of war, proclaimed the human right to life, the right of conscience and freedom, the supremacy of reason, the sanctity of work, and the blessings of peace. And, since the thrones of our monarchs cast us into darkness, let the tombs of these great thinkers restore us to the light!

II
The Lessons of Peace History

The above account of peace thinking from ancient times to the end of the 19th century is necessarily selective. It does not cover the history of heterodox pacifist thought which has been brilliantly rescued from obscurity by the peace historian Peter Brock (*Pacifism in Europe to 1914*, Princeton, 1972). Nor have I attempted to consider how peace has been regarded in the religious traditions of Islam and Buddhism – both areas where much research remains to be done. Yet my survey should be sufficient to dispel two common myths: either that concern for peace is a relatively modern conception, or that opposition to the war in the past was based on utopian or idealistic arguments of little relevance today. A further criticism also needs to be dealt with; that even if peace advocates in historical times did address practical issues, the character of war has changed to such an extent that what they had to say is of little relevance today. To this I would reply that while the character – or at least the form of war – has changed in some, (though not all) respects, the thinking which leads governments to opt for a military solution while rejecting or downgrading a peaceful alternative, and therefore to choose war as an instrument of policy, remains substantially unchanged. What Mengzi or Erasmus or Penn or Kant or Hugo or von Suttner had to say about peace is not only of great historical interest, but can also illuminate our own efforts to strive for the same goal. (If they had been listened to, we may suggest, there would have been no Iraq War!) A desire for peace has been woven into the fabric of human consciousness not just in recent times but throughout history, and knowledge of this rich historical record of peace thought and argument should sustain and encourage our own efforts.

The Benefits of Peace

Rejecting the view that war is in some way essential for human development, the peace thinkers of the past concur in their appreciation of the beneficial character of peace – indeed that the condition of peace is indispensable for the growth of civilisation. Peace, as Erasmus put it eloquently, is 'at once the mother and nurse of all that is good for humanity... Peace shines on human affairs like the sun in springtime'. St Augustine also wrote at length on the benefits of peace, linking this to the argument – fundamental to his philosophy – that human beings should live the best, and most peaceful, lives possible rather than simply wait for the life hereafter.

> *[God has] imparted to men some good things adapted to this life, to wit, temporal peace, such as we can enjoy in this life from health and safety and human fellowship, and all things needful for the preservation and recovery of this peace, such as the objects which are accommodated to our outward senses, light, night, the air, and waters suitable for us, and equitable condition, that every man who made a good use of these advantages suited to the peace of this mortal condition, should receive ampler and better blessings, namely, the peace of immortality, accompanied by glory and honour.*

Kant has a more sophisticated view of the role of peace in human development. He is no idealist (contrary to the charge laid against him by some war historians), and even asserts that the 'natural state' of humans living side by side 'is one of war'. But, he continues, humanity has now reached the level, through a process of repeated wars, at which the danger of continued war, and its adverse effect on economic development, will oblige the new nation-states to formulate and abide by international law, and that this should in time lead to global harmony and agreement.

Here we may see that Kant has anticipated Charles Darwin who – again contrary to popular misperception – believed that competition within the human species would, as civilisation evolved and as communities grew larger, give way to the realisation that co-operation could be a more effective driver for progress and development. The following passage from *The Descent of Man* should, I suggest, be a compulsory element in any discussion of Darwinism.

> *As man advances in civilisation, and small tribes are united into larger communities, the simplest reason would tell each individual that he ought to extend his social instincts and sympathies to all the members of the same nation, though personally unknown to him. This point being once reached, there is only an artificial barrier to prevent his sympathies extending to the men of all nations and races...*
>
> *This virtue, one of the noblest with which man is endowed, seems to arise*

incidentally from our sympathies becoming more tender and more widely diffused, until they are extended to all sentient beings. As soon as this virtue is honoured and practised by some few men, it spreads through instruction and example to the young, and eventually becomes incorporated in public opinion.

Peace theorists of the late 19th century, such as Jacques Novikow and Jean de Bloch, built upon Darwin's approach, seeking to show that peaceful economic competition had replaced armed conflict as man's principal activity, and pointing to the role of science and technology in promoting peaceful development. Here they were combating the arguments of the so-called Social Darwinists who distorted Darwin's own findings in order to assert 'the necessity of struggle', and who argued that war would continue to be the driving force for all human progress.

Education for Peace

Peace thinkers from the earliest time have understood the importance of persuasion: their rulers had to be convinced that the cost of war will almost always be higher than the cost of any compromise necessary to avoid war. As Erasmus put it in *The Education of a Christian Prince,* the effects of war are so damaging that the wise prince will 'sometimes prefer to lose a thing [by not fighting] than to gain it [through war]'. And even more bluntly in his *The Complaint of Peace*: 'hardly any peace is so bad that it is not preferable to the most justifiable war'. In modern terms, we might say this is a question of accurate cost-benefit analysis, with the problem that too often the short term gains of war are not properly measured against the long-term dis-benefits.

In seeking to persuade potential war-makers of the dangers of seeking 'peace through war', one also has to combat the arguments of those with a vested interest in arguing the opposite. The Confucian peace advocates of the Warring States period made no secret of their loathing for the Strategists and Legalists who urged their rulers to make war. 'The so-called good ministers of today [who advise their prince to go to war] would have been called robbers of the people in olden days,' commented Mengzi. His successor Xunzi, when asked by the ruler of his native state what was the best way for a king to manage his army, replied dismissively that 'such detailed matters are of minor importance to Your Majesty, and may be left to the generals'. Xunzi shared Mengzi's insistence that what was of real importance was to rule with humanity and justice, and that unity between the ruler and the people was the best way to resist aggression. 'For a tyrant to try to overthrow a good ruler by force would be like throwing eggs at a rock or stirring boiling water with your finger.'

Peace advocates of the Enlightenment, in the age when armies were becoming professional and the military establishment gained more power in the courts of the nation-states, recognised the growing strength of the vested interests for war, and the difficulty experienced by kings and princes in resisting their pressure. The dilemma was eloquently put by Denis Diderot, author of the great *Encyclopédie* (c. 1760), in which peace was given its own entry and definition:

> *The sovereign has need of unalterable firmness, and an invincible love of order and the public good, to resist the clamour of those warriors who surround him. Their tumultuous voice constantly stifles the cry of the nation whose sole interest lies in tranquillity. The partisans of war have no shortage of pretexts with which to stir up disorder and make their own self-interested wishes known.*

By the mid-19th century, the existence of what we would now describe, following President Eisenhower's warning, as the military-industrial establishment, was a stock theme in the discourse of the newly emerging peace societies. 'There is a large portion of the community which does not want peace,' warned Richard Cobden. 'War is the profession of some men, and war, therefore, is the only means for their occupation and promotion in their profession' (speech at Wrexham, November 1850).

Mediation for Peace

The advocates of peace have always recognised that it will not come by itself, that hard work is needed to avert conflict between rival parties, and that this will require a negotiated solution. St Augustine understood this very well, declaring that 'It is a higher glory still to stay war with a word, than to slay men with a sword, and to procure or maintain peace by peace, not by war'. Erasmus, too, had a very clear idea about the need for some form of mediation between those about to go to war:

> *There are laws, there are scholars, venerable abbots, reverend bishops, by whose prudent counsel the matter can be composed. Why not try these arbiters, who can hardly create more problems and are likely to cause many fewer than if recourse were had to the battlefield?*

As the new world order of nation-states began to take shape, peace advocates began to explore means of establishing more permanent mechanisms through which to mediate conflict and, if necessary, to enforce a settlement. William Penn's proposal for a pan-European council amounted to a permanent international tribunal, in which the European countries were represented by delegates in numbers corresponding to their economic power. Penn even anticipated modern conference procedure by setting out rules for the layout of the council chamber: the room should be round and entered by more than one door to prevent any quarrel over precedence. In his *Project for Perpetual Peace*, the Abbé de Saint Pierre proposed a League of European States with a permanent Congress of Representatives, and a Senate with powers to arbitrate disputes and enforce its decisions if necessary by military sanctions, while all peacetime armies were to be reduced in size to no more than 6,000. Kant also began to explore the relationship between individual states and the community of nations, proposing a 'federation' of states which could in theory 'lead to perpetual peace' – although in practice he conceded that this is unlikely to be achieved, and that we must settle for a more limited alliance to prevent specific wars.

The peace societies of the 19th century, while stressing the moral case against war, placed the main emphasis of their argument upon its economic irrationality, and on the possibility of resolving disputes by peaceful means – and, in particular, through international arbitration. In a modest early success, at the Paris conference which ended the Crimean war, a peace deputation led by Richard Cobden persuaded the delegates of the great powers to include in the treaty a protocol expressing the 'desire' for recourse to mediation in future disputes. The campaign to promote international arbitration as the way to settle disputes by peaceful means rather than by war was boosted by a provision in the 1871 Treaty of Washington between Great Britain and the United States in which a contentious issue (the 'Alabama dispute') was referred to an arbitration committee in Geneva. In Britain, Henry Richard, secretary of the Peace Society and a Liberal MP, scored a notable victory by proposing a parliamentary motion in favour of arbitration, and winning an unexpected majority:

> *While spending so much of time, thought, skill, and money in organizing war, is it not worth while to bestow some forethought and care in trying to organize peace, by making some provision beforehand for solving by peaceable means those difficulties and complications that arise to disturb the relations of States, instead of leaving them to the excited passions and hazardous accidents of the moment? (Hansard, 8 July 1873)*

By the end of the 19th century, peace activists could claim a share of credit for dozens of bilateral treaties and agreements between states with provisions for the peaceful arbitration of disputes. Plans for obligatory arbitration on a wider international scale, and for the creation of a real international judiciary, began to be discussed. Though optimism was already fading by the time of the second Hague Peace Conference in 1907, the peace societies had sown the seeds for a society of nations which, after the war, would germinate into the League of Nations (and in turn pave the way for the United Nations). Overall, these were significant gains.

The Globalisation of Peace

We have become increasingly familiar over the last century with the concept that peace is indivisible and that it is not enough to have the absence of war without freedom from oppression and hunger unless these advantages are shared by one's neighbours. This approach acquired a global reach in the post-Cold War period of the 1990s, with the concept of 'human security' promoted by the UN Development Programme in its Human Development Reports. It has been carried a stage further by the Oxford Research Group in formulating the concept of 'sustainable security', which addresses both the continuing inequalities of world society, and the new types of security threats of the 21st century. It has also been developed in the concept of 'cosmopolitan peace', proposed by the international historian Ken Booth, in which international security is promoted by humanising the powerful forces of economic globalisation which are already at work.

This notion of a cosmopolitan world in which harmony between peoples is the indispensable basis for peace was already familiar in the history of peace thinking. It can be found in the ideas of the Greek Cynics who believed (in words attributed to Diogenes of Sinope) that 'the only true commonwealth is one which is as wide as the universe'. It may be found, too, in the cosmopolitan world view of the Roman Stoics: thus Seneca describes the outline of a commonwealth of humanity which is:

> *A vast and truly common state, which embraces alike gods and men, in which we look neither to this corner of earth nor to that, but measure the bounds of our citizenship by the path of the sun.* (De Otio)

Erasmus and his fellow-humanists of the Renaissance were strongly influenced by this aspect of Stoic thought, and argued for what we would now call an internationalist approach to the regulation of human affairs. Juan Luis Vives, in his time as well-known as Erasmus, addressed Henry VIII in 1525 with a personal appeal for peace between England and France: 'My anxiety is great in seeing the Christian world divided by dissensions and wars, and it seems that a perturbation cannot be caused in any part of the world without affecting all the rest'. Vives went on to argue (*De Concordia*) that Concord or harmony was both natural and essential to human progress, whereas Discord or war was destructive, materially and spiritually, of all that made life worthwhile. Vives's proposal for promoting European concord has been described as a precursor of the concept of the League of Nations.

The narrative of peace, which extends from the humanists to the Enlightenment, increasingly focused on the need for international co-operation which transcended national and even continental boundaries. In an early example, Émeric Crucé's proposal for a Council of Ambassadors to resolve disputes between states included not only the European states but also 'the Emperor of the Turks, the Jews, the Kings of Persia and China, the Grand Duke of Moscovy (Russia) and monarchs from India and Africa'. In *Perpetual Peace*, Kant would write that 'a violation of rights in one place is felt throughout the world'. It followed that 'the idea of a law of world citizenship is no high-flown or exaggerated notion'.

By the 19th century, a strong theme of liberal internationalism permeates the arguments of peace advocacy (although complicated at times by the conflicting demand for national liberation). As well as emphasising the need for an international legal framework for peace, it has a strong humanitarian aspect – reflected in the foundation of the International Committee of the Red Cross. Much-quoted in later years, Victor Hugo's peroration to the first great Peace Conference (Paris, 1849) conveys the general feeling that national boundaries were being eroded by technological progress, and that this should create a sounder basis for universal peace. The day would come, he forecast, 'when there will be no battlefields other than markets open to trade and minds open to ideas. The day will come when cannon balls and bombs will be replaced by votes, by the universal suffrage of peoples', and by a 'supreme, sovereign senate' for the whole of Europe.

The very fact that peace societies, movements and leagues could be formed on a transnational basis, that they could collectively lobby world rulers, sometimes to good effect, and that support for concrete goals such as arbitration and disarmament could be gained, taking advantage of new mass communications, in the populations of many countries, strengthened the sense that peace was now an international enterprise. The rising tide of revolutionary socialism/Marxism, although it rejected what was regarded as bourgeois pacifism, coincided in the sense that it too envisaged action by the proletariat across national borders. The gap between the two was partly bridged at times – notably at the Stuttgart Congress of the Second International (1907), which urged the working-class to take strike action against the threat of war.

Bertha von Suttner, the Austrian peace pioneer who played an important part in mobilising support for the 1899 Peace Conference, would sum up the new mood of popular internationalism in her Nobel Peace Prize lecture (April 1906):

We must understand that two philosophies, two eras of civilization, are wrestling with one another and that a vigorous new spirit is supplanting the blatant and threatening old. No longer weak and formless, this promising new life is already widely established and determined to survive. Quite apart from the peace movement, which is a symptom rather than a cause of actual change, there is taking place in the world a process of internationalization and unification. Factors contributing to the development of this process are technical inventions, improved communications, economic interdependence, and closer international relations. The instinct of self-preservation in human society, acting almost subconsciously, as do all drives in the human mind, is rebelling against the constantly refined methods of annihilation and against the destruction of humanity.

The Popular Voice for Peace

Muffled for ages but never entirely silent, becoming more audible to our ears in the last two centuries, the role of ordinary people in rejecting war and seeking peace has always been present in human society, and was often acknowledged by the peace thinkers who are surveyed here. We hear it in the popular ballads collected for the Chinese *Book of Songs (Shijing)* in which, during the 'Spring and Autumn' period (722-403BC) of turbulent warfare, conscript soldiers and their dependants complain bitterly of separation, hardship, the destruction of families and the wasting of their land. In classical Athens where, as already noted, the voices of peace advocates in the Athenian Assembly remain silent in the orthodox history, a popular desire for peace breaks through upon the stage on which, through the medium of comedy, dissenting voices were allowed. In three of the surviving plays of Aristophanes (*The Acharnians, Peace,* and *Lysistrata*), we hear the authentic voice of the man and woman in the street when it has not been swayed by pro-war oratory. (*The Archanians*, an ancient commentary, noted 'appeals for peace in every possible way'). At the conclusion of *Peace,* its hero Trygaeus, a very ordinary Athenian, but one with more common sense than the generals, celebrates rumbustiously his success in liberating the goddess Peace from the heavenly cave into which she had been cast by War.

> *Remember, lads, the life of old*
> *Which Peace put in our way:*
> *The myrtle, figs and little cakes,*
> *The luscious fruit all day,*
> *The violet banks and olive groves,*
> *All things for which we sigh,*
> *Peace has now brought back to us,*
> *So greet her with joyous cry!*

Medieval Europe is not usually associated with anti-militarism, yet large-scale demonstrations for peace did occur when the populace was driven to protest by the endless round of oppression and war. This popular voice was usually mediated through the accounts of literate clerics who might not always be in sympathy with it, or might exploit it for different ends. In the Peace of God (*pax dei*) movement of the late 10th to 11th centuries, the Church encouraged popular backing for its attempts to place limits on the marauding greed of warlord nobles who often encroached on ecclesiastical privilege. Thousands of the common folk, we are told by the chroniclers, gathered at assemblies called by the bishops, and cried out to God for 'Peace, Peace, Peace!'

Non-conformist religious movements such as the Cathars and Albigenses, the Penitents and Flagellants, and (in England) the Lollards, voiced pacifist views although not always consistently, and their voices were also distorted by accusations against them of heresy. The Tenth Conclusion of the Lollards' manifesto, nailed to the door of Parliament in 1395, was directed against 'War, Battle and Crusades'. John Wyclif had already criticised the Pope for approving of the Crusades – for the Pope, says Wyclif, may sin as much as anyone else. Medieval literature also offers insights into arguments which countered the dominant values of militarism and chivalry (itself an ambiguous concept). In the words of the Norman cleric Guillaume le Clerc, expressed in his allegorical poem *Le Besant de Dieu* (1227):

> *God! how shall a Christian king send forth from his kingdom thirty thousand fighting men, who must leave their bereaved wives and children at home, when they go into mortal combats in which a thousand shall soon be slain and never again see their country, and as many men on the other side.*

Popular anti-war sentiment in the age of modern warfare from the 18th into the 19th century was often drowned out by the sound of drums and the display of scarlet uniforms as princely regimes sought to mobilise the populace for cannon fodder. However, with the spread of literacy and modern communications, the Napoleonic Wars initiated a new awareness of the real horrors of armed – and still mostly hand-to-hand – conflict. 19th century writers such as Stendhal (*The Charterhouse of Parma*), Thackeray (*Vanity Fair*), Zola (*La Débâcle*) and, most famously, Tolstoy in his *War and Peace*, presented an emphatically anti-heroic view of war. The mass media of the 19th century also began to report, though usually in a form biased in favour of the colonial powers, the popular resistance of many colonised peoples. The full extent of such resistance, which typically began with passive and non-violent disaffection but, when suppressed by violence, was likely to become violent in return, is still not sufficiently recognised. (Richard Gott's *Britain's Empire: Resistance, repression and revolt,* Verso, 2011, fills an important gap in this story.) Gandhi is often credited with virtually inventing the concept of non-violent protest, yet it must have been practised in many thousands of separate incidents in Europe, Africa and Asia for many centuries.

The popular voice for peace, as we are well aware, has become louder and clearer in the last hundred years although it still can be swayed by appeals to patriotism and chauvinism. Yet from ancient times onwards, peace thinkers have recognised that peace is, in the end, about serving the interests of the people, and that peace is more likely to be secured if the people can be rallied to its cause. Although we live today in very different times, the validity of this proposition is not diminished, and we have seen important (though unfortunately not yet sufficient) results from popular activism against war and nuclear weapons. I could conclude this article with a suitable quotation on the subject from one of the great peace advocates of the modern world, such as Jane Addams, Albert Einstein, Bertrand Russell, Joseph Rotblat, Alva Myrdal, Johan Galtung or Kenneth Boulding. Instead, I shall end with a lyric from a popular song of the mid-19th century, often sung in the music-halls of Britain. The singer is a young woman, saying farewell to her lover who is going off to the wars, and the last four lines of her ballad, widely quoted at the time by the advocates of peace, convey a simple and still important truth.

> *When glory leads the way, you'll be madly rushing on,*
> *Never thinking if they kill you that my happiness is gone.*
> *If you win the day perhaps, a general you'll be;*
> *Though I'm proud to think of that, what will become of me!*
> *Oh, if I were Queen of France – or, still better, Pope of Rome,*
> *I would have no fighting men abroad – no weeping maids at home.*
> *All the world should be at peace, or if kings must show their might,*
> *Why, let them who make the quarrel be the only men to fight.*
>
> ('Jeannette's Song', c .1848)

With grateful acknowledgements to the Oxford Research Group
www.oxfordresearchgroup.org

Opportunities Lost

Ban Ki-moon

Ban Ki-moon is the Secretary General of the United Nations. He published this sobering assessment on 28 August 2012 as he attended the Non-Aligned Movement Summit in Tehran.

In July 2012, competing interests prevented agreement on a much-needed treaty that would have reduced the appalling human cost of the poorly regulated international arms trade. Meanwhile, nuclear disarmament efforts remain stalled, despite strong and growing global popular sentiment in support of this cause.

The failure of these negotiations and August's anniversaries of the atomic bombings at Hiroshima and Nagasaki provide a good opportunity to explore what has gone wrong, why disarmament and arms control have proven so difficult to achieve, and how the world community can get back on track towards these vitally important goals.

Many defence establishments now recognize that security means far more than protecting borders. Grave security concerns can arise as a result of demographic trends, chronic poverty, economic inequality, environmental degradation, pandemic diseases, organized crime, repressive governance and other developments no state can control alone. Arms can't address such concerns.

Yet there has been a troubling lag between recognizing these new security challenges, and launching new policies to address them. National budget priorities still tend to reflect the old paradigms. Massive military spending and new investments in modernizing nuclear weapons have left the world over-armed and peace under-funded.

Last year, global military spending reportedly exceeded $1.7 trillion, more than $4.6 billion a day, which alone is almost twice the UN's budget for an entire year.

This largesse includes billions more for modernizing nuclear arsenals decades into the future.

This level of military spending is hard to explain in a post-Cold War world and amidst a global financial crisis. Economists would call this an 'opportunity cost'. I call it human opportunities lost. Nuclear weapons budgets are especially ripe for deep cuts. Such weapons are useless against today's threats to international peace and security. Their very existence is de-stabilizing: the more they are touted as indispensable, the greater is the incentive for their proliferation. Additional risks arise from accidents and the health and environmental effects of maintaining and developing such weapons. The time has come to re-affirm commitments to nuclear disarmament, and to ensure that this common end is reflected in national budgets, plans and institutions.

Four years ago, I outlined a five-point disarmament proposal highlighting the need for a nuclear weapon convention or a framework of instruments to achieve this goal. Yet the disarmament stalemate continues. The solution clearly lies in greater efforts by States to harmonize their actions to achieve common ends. Here are some specific actions that all States and civil society should pursue to break this impasse.

- Support efforts by the Russian Federation and the United States to negotiate deep, verified cuts in their nuclear arsenals, both deployed and un-deployed.
- Obtain commitments by others possessing such weapons to join the disarmament process.
- Establish a moratorium on developing or producing nuclear weapons or new delivery systems.
- Negotiate a multilateral treaty outlawing fissile materials that can be used in nuclear weapons.
- End nuclear explosions and bring into force the Comprehensive Nuclear-Test-Ban Treaty.
- Ensure that nuclear-weapon states report to a public UN repository on nuclear disarmament, including details on arsenal size, fissile material, delivery systems, and progress in achieving disarmament goals.
- Establish a Middle East zone free of nuclear weapons and other weapons of mass destruction.
- Secure universal membership in treaties outlawing chemical and biological weapons.
- Pursue parallel efforts on conventional arms control, including an arms trade treaty, strengthened controls over the illicit trade in small arms and light weapons, universal membership in the Mine Ban, Cluster Munitions, and Inhumane Weapons Conventions, and expanded

participation in the UN Report on Military Expenditures and the UN Register of Conventional Arms.

- Undertake diplomatic and military initiatives to maintain international peace and security in a world without nuclear weapons, including new efforts to resolve regional disputes.
- And perhaps above all, we must address basic human needs and achieve the Millennium Development Goals. Chronic poverty erodes security. Let us dramatically cut spending on nuclear weapons, and invest instead in social and economic development, which serves the interests of all by expanding markets, reducing motivations for armed conflicts, and in giving citizens a stake in their common futures. Like nuclear disarmament and non-proliferation, such goals are essential for ensuring human security and a peaceful world for future generations.

No development, no peace. No disarmament, no security. Yet when both advance, the world advances, with increased security and prosperity for all. These are common ends that deserve the support of all nations.

New type of US nuclear test

Nagasaki protests

Japan's southwestern city of Nagasaki expressed its outrage and protest against a new type of nuclear test conducted for the sixth time in August 2012 by the United States, the local press reported. The report said that the United States conducted a nuclear test which simulated a nuclear blast using intense X-ray beams and checked how plutonium would react at the Sandia National Laboratories in New Mexico on 27 August. The sixth test caused further condemnation by the city, following earlier protests against the fifth new type of nuclear test which was reportedly carried out between April and June this year.

According to the report, Nagasaki Mayor Tomihisa Taue sent a letter of protest, dated 24 September 2012, to US President Barack Obama, saying that the people of Nagasaki, who have been calling for the elimination of nuclear weapons, cannot restrain their resentment after encountering reports about a further test despite their protest. 'As a representative of an atomic-bombed city I strongly protest again,' the mayor said. The letter also urged that the United States make sincere efforts to stop any nuclear tests, adding that the country should fulfil its leadership role in achieving a world without nuclear weapons.

Xinhua News Agency 25 September 2012

Assembly line for disarmament

Sergio Duarte

In February 2012, Ambassador Duarte retired as UN High Representative for Disarmament Affairs, ending his distinguished tenure of this demanding and difficult office. He had become a familiar figure to activists in the cause of peace and disarmament, regularly travelling the globe to speak at CND's conference in London or representing the UN Secretary General in Hiroshima and Nagasaki at the annual Conference Against A and H Bombs. He made himself accessible, and there was always substance to what he said, as indicated in these excerpts from his statement to the First Committee of the UN General Assembly, responsible for Disarmament and International Security, when it met in New York in October 2011.

By any measure, this Committee has on its agenda some of the most difficult challenges for international peace and security. Its deliberations will cover the world's deadliest weapons of mass destruction, including the most indiscriminate of all, nuclear weapons. It will address issues relating to the regulation and limitation of conventional arms. And it will take up other subjects that have profound implications for our common future – including space weapons, the relationship between disarmament and development, disarmament education, regional co-operation, and issues relating to institutions in the United Nations disarmament machinery.

We are all familiar with the extent that progress in disarmament depends on its broader political climate. Some have argued that this political climate alone determines both the rate of progress and its future prospects. There is some truth in this, but opinions differ over which trends are producing which results, and many are not convinced that the environment determines disarmament outcomes, and not the other way around.

Some claim, for example, that if there is no peace or stability, if armed conflicts continue, if regional disputes remain unresolved, and if risks of weapons proliferation or terrorism persist – then under such circumstances, there can be no disarmament.

If this argument were true, one might conclude that this Committee would be well advised to adjourn today, because all our work would be held hostage to developments occurring outside the walls of this chamber. Our role would amount to little more than to echo those trends.

Yet there is another view of the role of this Committee that I believe has been more widely accepted over its last sixty-five years. This view holds that the Committee has the capability to make its own independent contribution to advancing multilateral norms in disarmament and, thereby, to strengthening international peace and security. This Committee did not halt its work even during the darkest years of the Cold War, when nuclear arsenals were growing and threats of nuclear war were not uncommon and widely recognized as such – so much so, they became the subject of popular novels and films.

Let us recall that most of the multilateral treaties that currently exist were negotiated during a geopolitical era marked by arms races, regional wars, and an intense multidimensional rivalry between the world's two great Superpowers. How could this have been possible if progress in disarmament had first to satisfy the preconditions of world peace and stability?

Today, we are fortunate to be conducting our deliberations in a substantially improved political climate. The Cold War has now been over for an entire generation. While over 20,000 nuclear weapons remain – and their operational status is unclear – the size of those arsenals has fallen considerably since their estimated peak of over 70,000 around 1986. More impressively, popular attitudes towards such weapons have also been changing in recent decades. In particular, the humanitarian consequences of the use of these weapons have been receiving greater recognition – as reflected in the 1996 Advisory Opinion of the International Court of Justice, in statements and work of the International Committee of the Red Cross, and most recently in language adopted by consensus in the 2010 Nuclear Non-Proliferation Treaty Review Conference.

Equally impressive has been the increasing variety of actors who are working around the world for global nuclear disarmament, and this includes an active role by the Secretary-General, who in 2010 became the first Secretary-General to visit Hiroshima and Nagasaki. In March 2011, I was proud to join him in opening a new display at the UN's Disarmament Exhibition showing twin stacks of a petition for a nuclear weapons convention – that petition had over a million signatures collected by Mayors for Peace, an organization representing over 5000 cities in 151 countries. Another international petition, also in support of such a convention, was presented by the Japanese group Gensuikyo at the NPT Review Conference – and it had over 7 million signatures.

In addition to city mayors and grass-roots organizations, national parliamentarians have also been taking an increased interest in promoting progress in nuclear disarmament. In April 2009, the Assembly of the Inter-Parliamentary Union – representing 600 parliamentarians from over 100 countries – adopted a resolution that also supported negotiation of a nuclear weapons convention, as originally proposed by Secretary-General Ban Ki-moon on 24 October 2008. And in September 2009, the UN Security Council – after decades of not addressing this issue – held a summit meeting that produced Resolution 1887, which called upon all States, not just the parties to the NPT, to enter into good faith negotiations on nuclear disarmament.

As we consider these facts – while recognizing the uncertainties of the future – it is possible to observe two reinforcing trends that could positively influence the work of this Committee both this year and in the years ahead. The first is the trend associated with the democratic revolution now sweeping the world, not just the Middle East. Evidence that democracy is coming to disarmament is indisputable in the actions I have just cited by the mayors, parliamentarians, and civil society groups throughout the world. It is apparent in the persisting and growing expectations voiced in the General Assembly for new progress in disarmament – and as the world's largest democratic body, the General Assembly offers a forum for each State, large or small, to participate in the process of developing multilateral disarmament norms.

And as democracy is coming to disarmament, so too is the rule of law. This is apparent in the persisting efforts to gain universal membership in the key multilateral treaties dealing with weapons of mass destruction – the Biological Weapons Convention, the Chemical Weapons Convention, and the Nuclear Non-Proliferation Treaty. It is apparent in strong and, I believe, growing interest in support of negotiating a nuclear weapons convention, or at least for serious consideration of what types of legal obligations would be necessary to achieve a world free of nuclear weapons. It is apparent in recent meetings by the nuclear-weapon States to consult on ways to improve transparency of their nuclear arsenals and stocks of fissile materials, a longstanding goal of the world community. It is apparent in the importance the entire world attaches to full compliance with disarmament and non-proliferation commitments. It is apparent in efforts to prevent an arms race in outer space, to agree on norms governing missiles and missile defences, and to strengthen international legal obligations in the field of non-proliferation and against terrorism involving weapons of mass destruction. And it is apparent in efforts that have been underway since the 2010 NPT Review Conference to pursue the establishment of a weapons-of-mass-destruction-free zone in the Middle East – and such efforts will hopefully produce progress quite soon.

These twin forces of democracy and the rule of law also have the potential to help in achieving another longstanding goal – namely, a reduction in military spending, or in the words of Article 26 of the UN Charter, 'the least diversion for armaments of the world's human and economic resources'. At present the world is reportedly spending over $1.6 trillion a year for military purposes, while progress in achieving many of the great Millennium Developments Goals has fallen short of expectations given the lack of resources.

In terms of the work of this Committee, it is therefore quite clear that we should not close up shop and wait for the dawning of world peace as a precondition for disarmament, non-proliferation and arms control to succeed. To the contrary, our efforts in each of these fields make their own vital and independent contributions in strengthening international peace and security. And as disarmament advances, the world advances.

Our efforts offer prospects for reducing mistrust in the world. Arms reductions can help not only in reducing regional tensions, but in eliminating the likelihood of large-scale armed conflicts. Far from affirming the legality or utility of nuclear weapons for national or collective self-defence, nuclear disarmament efforts satisfy both the law and the will of the people, while also enhancing security far more reliably than a precarious balance of nuclear terror.

For all these reasons, disarmament remains a goal shared by all Member States. What is most needed now is the political will to translate these goals into action. For this work to be undertaken on a global scale there is no substitute for the UN disarmament machinery as a venue for multilateral co-operation. It remains the world's great 'assembly line' for the construction and maintenance of global disarmament norms. As the forces of democracy continue to grow, so too will the legitimacy of international rules in this field – and as the rule of law continues to come to disarmament, so too will the world welcome the additional stability, predictability, and basic fairness that will arise as a result.

In short, democracy and the rule of law are two powerful forces in the global environment that together can help strengthen the political will needed to move the disarmament agenda forward.

I wrote *March Time* in 1987 and revised it in 1994. It was commissioned by Stewart McKinnon of Trade Films for Channel 4, but in the end was never made.

It is now in the process of being adapted for live performance. Red Ladder Theatre Company hope to produce it in autumn 2013 at Building 21 in Elsecar Heritage Centre near Barnsley.

The text published here is the original screenplay. Readers who wish to know more about its writing may be interested in the arresting chapter on *March Time* in John Tulloch's book *Trevor Griffiths*, published by Manchester University Press in 2006.

Trevor Griffiths, September 2012

Illustration: Grateful acknowledgements to Ray Lowry and Leeds Postcards

March Time

an original screenplay by Trevor Griffiths

*For Ken,
mentor
comrade
godfather
friend*

*Men of England, wherefore plough
For the lords who lay you low?
Wherefore weave with toil and care
The rich robes your tyrants wear?*

*The seed ye sow, another reaps;
The wealth ye find, another keeps;
The robe ye weave, another wears;
The arms ye forge, another bears ...*
        Shelley: *Song to the Men of England*

*Black. Fade up Dunn's voice, speaking
quietly.*

DUNN: ... My lord, I will not waste your
time with pleas of mitigation, you have
found me guilty and will sentence me as
you see fit. But this I will say. The
fellow workers I am supposed to have
assaulted were no such thing, but the
worthless gobs of vomit we call scabs,
fished from the cess-pits of the world by
hard-hearted coal barons to steal our
jobs and break our spirit ... (*Applause,
cheers from Gallery. The Judge's gavel;
his calls for silence*) And the so-called
police officers I'm supposed to have
obstructed were no such thing, but
agents of the owning class carrying out
the work of their masters ...

*Stormy applause. Courtroom, Durham
Assizes. The judge gavels for silence from
the agitated gallery packed with the
prisoner's pit-mates.*

*Close shot Dunn, the prisoner, 44, dark,
contained, scanning them from the dock.
He exchanges a wan smile with Gypsy
Armstrong, a heavy man around 40 with
an earring and strange 19th century
pitman's pigtail. Lands finally on a black-
haired woman, late 30s, her arm round her*

son's shoulder, her gaze back at him hard and unyielding.

Silence is restored. The judge resumes his judicious sifting of papers.

DUNN: … As to contrition, my lord, I will not feign what I do not feel. For if a freeborn Englishman, in lawful union with his peers, may not defend his work and his community without incurring the wrath of the courts, then this is indeed a sorry land, and I and many like me will not rest until these things are changed. We are already too many for your prisons, each day we grow in numbers and resolve. And we will make this <u>our</u> century, building peace and fairness where now there is only strife and greed. And there will <u>be</u> better days …

The gallery erupts with feeling. The judge gavels and flutes for silence. Dunn looks across at the woman, who shakes her head tautly in the gloom, buries her face in her hands.

Sound fades very slowly, movement slows, as the sentence is delivered – six months with hard labour – and Dunn is handcuffed and returned to the cells.

Fade to black.

Fade up a woman's voice:

WOMAN: *(letter voice)* … I suppose I know now you'll not change, not you, but I'm still young enough to start over, and that's what I'll do. But I'm not one to hide behind letters, Jack, so if you want to come and talk it out, you'll know where to find me …

Fade up still image of long empty stretch of country lane in long shot.

Caption: <u>March, 1927.</u>

After some moments, a figure crests a rise in the far distance, headed for camera, a rolled kit-bag on his shoulder.

Bring up sounds of a six-piece pit band tuning up. The advancing figure, still distant, holds the road alone for some while, then others appear, by twos and threes, optically inserted, till the lane's dense with marching figures. The crowded way gradually thins back to the solitary marcher, now almost at lane's end: it's Dunn, head prison-cropped, eyes fierce.

The pit band slides gently into The Internationale, *the camera follows the man into the approach to the village of Easley, where band and comrades are out in strength to greet his return. Sounds fade, movements slow; fade to black.*

Early morning over the pit village of Easley. Still images of limestone pit cottages, slagheaps, the stilled winding-wheel, the notice of closure on the colliery gates.

On the thin splash of green at the heart of the place, a group of men are erecting a rough platform. DMF banners, placards, posters, go up. Two men secure a high start-line banner on two poles proclaiming the Unemployed Workers National March on London (Easley Contingent).

Cut to close shot of a road map of Britain. A man's hand traces a route north to south.

DUNN: *(voice over)* ... The Scots set out last week, we'll meet up with them here ... *(a cross goes in, some way south)* ... fifty men, maybe a hundred ... Then we march down to here ... *(another cross)* to collect the Yorkshire lads ... and on down through Notts ... *(the pencil slides west into Lancashire)* ... The Lankies'll come down like this and rendezvous here *(a cross for Oxford)* with the Welshmen ... and ... *(the pencil draws lines of convergence)* with organization and a bit of luck, all twenty thousand of us'll fetch up here ... *(the pencil slashes London, a harsh tear of the lead)* ... Questions?

Cut to wide shot of kitchen, cramped miner's terraced cottage. Dunn stands by the map on the table, three men sit round it: Andy Armstrong (Gyp), with the pig-tail; Will Daly, tough, grayhaired, Scots, around 50; and Percy Mann, a retired pitman around 66. There are mugs of tea on the go; Gyp's on brown from a bottle; their bags and gear lie in a heap by the door.

DALY: Who're the two comin' from Wirkley Main, do we know?

DUNN: *(checking list)* ... Ray Douglas ...

MANN: *(coughing throughout)* Jimmie's lad. Aye ...

DUNN: ... Frank Pearson ... *(no one appears to know him)* They'll meet us by Salterton ... Cough's bad, Percy. You going to be up to this ...?

MANN: Just dust. No bother.

GYP: *(draining bottle, ready for off)* S'that it? Ah got some jobs to look to before we ...

DUNN: Hold on, Gyp. *(He looks at each of them in turn, as he hands out forms)* Read 'em, sign 'em, hand 'em in to the Lodge Secretary before we leave ... *(Armstrong's scanning his frowningly, lips on the move)*

… The National Organizing Committee's Rules of the March … No rowdiness, no fighting, no drunkenness, no stealing or general law-breaking.

GYP: … Bloody 'ell …

DUNN: We're passing though England, comrades, that other England, down there, as representatives of our class, disciplined, responsible, proud. And whatever the provocations of the State and its lackeys on the way, we will behave with dignity and cohesion … *(He returns to the mantelpiece as if finished, fishing for a pipe)* … Oh, and as section leader I'll not hesitate to sack <u>anyone</u> who steps out of line … *(He smiles, still serious)* … See you on the Green …

The men nod, gather their gear; Mann and Daly leave. Gyp hovers, adjusting the straps on his haversack. Dunn has lit his pipe, stares moodily at the family snaps on the mantelpiece – father, mother; the woman from the courtroom with a baby in her arms; their wedding photograph. The slow pan rests on an envelope propped against the clock: it bears his name, c/o Durham Gaol.

GYP: *(soft)* Have you heard from her?

Dunn shakes his head once; doesn't turn. Silence.

DUNN: *(eventually)* She's back with her folks. Lancashire. The lad too.

GYP: Aye. I heard. A tough lady. A woman of her word. *(Silence)* Can't blame 'er, though, eh? *(Dunn looks at him)* Who'd wanna live wi' the likes of us?

They smile, share something. Gyp shoulders his bag, heads for the back door, talking as he goes.

GYP: … Oh listen, if ah'm not there at nine, start without me, ah'll meet you over by Turley Bridge, ah've a lot on this mornin' …

Dunn frowns, goes to call him back, but he's away. Smiles. Crosses to the front room for his bags and gear. Slow scan of the book-packed walls, as he selects his reading for the trip: a worker-intellectual's library. He carries his gear to the kitchen. Takes the envelope down from the mantel, returns to the map on the table, studies it a moment longer as he fiddles the letter out.

Close shot of the map. A gold wedding-band drops, spins, settles on the maze of roadways. Close shot of Dunn's face staring at it.

Cut to

Long shot of Easley Green, filling with pitfolk. Fragments of the Lodge Secretary's speech of send-off drift across the dull air, much of it lost in the bark of dogs, the squeal of kids at play.

SECRETARY: ... All right, we lost the great battle of '26, some say betrayed by our leaders. But the war goes on. Their weapons now are unemployment, more hunger and starvation, more retrenchment of the services that make life possible for working men and women, more cuts in benefit and poor relief ... Well, we're sending a message down to those people ... Jack Dunn and the lads'll carry it, as will thousands upon thousands of others from all over this land. *(Voice lifting into passion)* We will not be broken. We will fight to the death for what we know to be ours: the right to work; and the right to the fruits of our labour. *(Cheers, applause)* Go well, bonnie lads. And godspeed.

More cheering, applause. Cut to

Closer shot of folk pressing small gifts of socks, tea, baccy, cakes and the like on the three-man contingent at the start-banner. The lodge secretary puffs frowningly down from the platform.

SECRETARY: What game on? Where's Gypsy Armstrong, Jack?

DUNN: *(collecting his walking staff)* Said he had something on, Albert. Meeting us at the bridge ... *(To others)* We ready?

SECRETARY: I fought agin' 'im goin', you know. Too bloody footloose ...

DUNN: He'll be fine, Albert. We'll be seeing you ...

Dunn lifts his staff. The full pit-band ahead strikes up with The Durham Miners Big Meeting *and marches the section off through the town. Kids and dogs trail them; drop away as the buildings end. The band breaks step. Instruments are lowered. The master calls Three Cheers. The three march on.*

Sound fades, movement slows. Fade to black.

Fade up

Vertical shot of blue and white blustery sky. At its exact centre, a hawk hovers, dead still on the wind. Cut to

Gyp, stretched out in a small pony cart, clay pipe smouldering, eyes fixed on the bird.

Dunn, Daly and Mann stride down the country lane, slow as they approach the ancient, peeling cart half-blocking the bridge. Smoke billows upwards from it. The older men stop, Dunn moves warily forward. Peers in over the side.

DUNN: What's this?

Gyp points to the bird. Dunn looks. The hawk glides lazily away.

GYP: Ah've watched that bugger every day for a week. Ah reckon he has a fine life … *(Dunn slaps the side of the cart. Gyp sits up, grins at the older men as they join Dunn)* This? This is gonna save our lives, bonnie lads.

DUNN: How?

GYP: *(standing)* Carry the gear, man.

Dunn looks at the others. Heads are shaken.

DUNN: *(patient)* And if we put the gear in there, somebody's going t'have to pull it …

Gyp grins, stands, finger and thumb to lips; whistles, one short, one long. A squeal from somewhere. Silence. A white pit pony, old, chubby, crashes out from beneath the bridge, trots up the bank, snorts to a halt in the road ahead of them, its near-blind head bobbing.

GYP: Old Billy, Jack. Lifted 'im out the knacker's van, day they closed us down … Ah've 'ad 'im out 'ere ever sin' …

Dunn looks at the others. They're both grinning.

DUNN: *(somewhere between grin and anger)* … He's a hundred and thirty, man, and half blind … What're you gonna do, tie his tail to the shafts …?

Gyp has stooped, comes up with a handful of home-made bridle and harness. Taps his nose. Shows his teeth.

Cut to

Noon. Outskirts of small pit-village. A signpost proclaims Salterton. We see the sides of the cart for the first time: a travelling hoarding for the March on London, all in Gyp's bold and rather crazy hand.

Ahead, a young woman, 25 maybe, slim, fair, a pack at her feet, dressed to walk, steps out from the side of the road to meet them. When she speaks, the voice is educated working-class Derbyshire.

WOMAN: Jack Dunn?

DUNN: *(wary)* Aye.

WOMAN: I've come from Wirkley.

DUNN: Aye? *(He studies her carefully; takes in the tension in her face: the dark sleep-bruises beneath the eyes: the black tie-band around her forehead)* And what's the news?

WOMAN: Ray Douglas came with me, but he turned back. Too shamed to tell you, he said. His wife and bab're both taken sick, and he'll not march.

DUNN: *(taking it in)* And Pearson?

WOMAN: Frank died three days back. We buried him this morning.

DUNN: Christ. *(pause)* I was told he was a young man …

WOMAN: So he was. Now he's as old as he's ever going to get. I'm his widow.

Silence. Dunn looks back at the others. When he looks at her again, the woman has picked up her back-pack and is wrestling it on. Dunn moves to help her, but she shrugs him away, finishes the job for herself.

WOMAN: Shall we go?

DUNN: *(slowly)* Go? Look, ma'am, I can see this has been a terrible loss for you, but it isn't a country ramble we're engaged …

WOMAN: … Mr Dunn. *(He stops)* Please don't patronize me, I know very well what this is. I'd like to join you.

Billy snickers, uneasy. Gyp chuckles. Percy Mann shushes him. Will Daly moves forward to join Dunn and the woman.

DALY: Missus, we're aiming to cover fifteen, twenty miles a day, living rough a lotta the time, on twopence a man a day plus what we can scrounge from the Guardians … *(gentle)* I know grief, ma'am. I lost my woman a year back and it still hurts. But this is men's work. You don't have to <u>do</u> this …

The woman nods, looks at each of the four in turn, ends on Dunn. Mann's coughing again, a slow dry persistence.

WOMAN: I can cook, I can chop wood, light fires, sew and darn … I have Frank's club money for the journey and I've lived on less than a shilling a week all my life … I've read the Rules of the March, and I agree to abide by them. If I can't keep up, sack me. But don't tell me this is men's work. Men've said it all my life and look where it's got us. My dad lived it … and died of dust before he reached fifty. I'm not going to apologise for being a woman. Women are workers too, part of the class, part of the suffering, part of the struggle. *(to Daly)* You're right. I don't have to do this. I choose to. *(pause)* And it's not grief makes me. It's anger. *(She steps back suddenly, to give them the road)* All right. The highways are free. I'll just follow behind …

Long silence. Dunn pokes his staff in the shale of the road.

DUNN: *(eventually)* Gyp.

GYP: Aye, Jack.

DUNN: *(slowly)* Put the lady's bag in the back, will you.

The woman nods at Dunn, removes her pack, hands it to Gyp. Dunn watches her, eyes dark, face wary.

DALY: *(behind him again)* Jack …

DUNN: *(eyes still on the woman)* Aye, I know, Will. I know.

The caravan sets up again. The woman takes her place with Gyp and Billy at the rear. Slow mix through to

Actuality film. Slowed bleached sequence of hunger marchers from 20s and 30s: banners, demands, programmes, thin faces, resolute eyes. Over this, possibly, the voices of those who marched, bearing witness.

Night. Derelict loose-box, on the edge of high farmland, South Durham. Cold rain drizzles through the half-gone roof. The sodden five huddle around a small woodfire. Gyp tends Percy Mann's blistered feet with delicate hands. Daly prepares the evening meal: cheese, boiled potatoes in their skins, brown bread, tea. Mrs Pearson lies on her side, back to the fire, eyes open. Jack Dunn writes up his log by the light of his miner's lamp.

DUNN: *(Journal voice over)* Fourth day. Marched twelve hours in poor weather. Percy's feet are bad and the woman's all in. But we've given ourselves a real chance of meeting the Scots boys the day after tomorrow as planned. *(He stops writing; watches the others a moment; exchanges a thin smile with Gyp; writes on.)* The police active again today. Six of them escorted us through Shotley Bridge and would not let us stop and hold a meeting for the unemployed there. One of them asked me if it was true we planned to blow up Parliament and start a revolution … Which has set me to thinking – if a few thousand determined men can cause this much panic, what might a <u>million</u> of us not achieve …?

He closes his book on the pencil, to take the proferred mug of tea from Daly, the food he's doled him. Gyp and Mann dig in, hungry. Mrs Pearson sits up slowly, stares at plate and mug laid out before her. Dunn studies her downturned face. Tears have dried in stains on her cheeks. Billy whinnies outside. Cut to

Night. Shot of the loose box. The half-door opens and Gyp looms out, a lamp in his hand. He walks towards the pony, tethered by a wall for shelter. The rain's stopped, the air's wet but mild. The man scratches the pony's chin as he stares out across the vast, barely visible plain below. Smells the air.

GYP: Smell it, Billy? *(He takes it in again)* Spring. That's what it is.

Man and pony stand there, taking it in.

Loose-box. Mann and Daly lie in their blankets by a wall. Mann wheezes heavily in his sleep. Dunn's propped against a wall, studies a map, his lamp on a nail above his right shoulder. Mrs Pearson has a book in her lap; stirs the fire for light.

DUNN: *(quiet)* What do you read?

WOMAN: Poetry. Shelley. *(He nods)* Not your cup of tea, I suppose …

Dunn makes no answer, head alert at random noises outside somewhere. The woman returns to her book. He returns to her eventually.

DUNN: We join up with the Scots lads Friday. Whoever leads them'll lead us down … *(She looks up at him)* They may not want you along, Ellen.

WOMAN: We'll see. *(Pause)* How do you know my name?

DUNN: Gypsy gave it me. You're a teacher, he says.

WOMAN: Was. Came up here last year from Derbyshire to take up my first post. Met Frank and married him. Three months later they closed the school. Three months after that they closed the pit.

He nods, eyes serious. She returns to her book.

DUNN: *(softly)* 'One. The majority of the people of England are destitute and miserable, ill-clothed, ill-fed, ill-educated. Two. The majority of the people of England know this and are impatient to procure a reform of the cause of their abject and wretched state. Three. The cause of this peculiar misery is unequal distribution which has been surreptitiously made of the products of their labour; for all property is the produce of labour. Four. The cause of that cause is a defect in government.' *(Pause. She stares at him wondering)* Analysis of the Condition of England, 1819. Prose, I'm afraid. But Shelley, nonetheless …

A long silence. Dunn returns to his map, pipe to mouth. The woman watches him across the fire.

Close shot of Dunn's map. It's of Europe. A pencil mark joins Harwich to Bremerhaven. His pencil extends the line: Berlin, Warsaw, Moscow. Cut to

Slow winding track in on man and pony, deep in conversation.

GYP: … Aye, well, ah'll grant it's a hard 'un for ye to grasp, Billy, you bein' a horse, but when they deny a man his work, his means of life, that's a slow sentence of death they pass on him, you see … For no crime, mind. Just for bein' poor … *(He's fishing in his pocket for a chew of baccy; the pony's head dips for it.)* … Hey, you wait your turn, you little divil …

He bites off his chew, the pony takes the rest. They savour it in silence under the black, star-filled sky. Mix slowly through to

Road. Afternoon. The five have been stopped by something in their path. They stare at it in silence, breath white on the cold air. A remote crackling hiss of voice comes from the thing they watch.

Reverse shot reveals an armoured car in the road ahead, staring straight at them, perhaps abandoned. A long moment. Dunn finally signals On. They edge past it with care. Billy shies as he passes. Gyp soothes him. Close shot of wireless cans hung on steering wheel: a BBC news announcer gives barely intelligible details of the Wall Street Crash.

Cut to

Day; fine, warm, gentle, the first of spring. Slow wide lens pan of South Durham countryside ends on shot of small town nestling below.

DUNN: *(over)* That's her. We'll spruce up and put on a show …

Woodland pool. Gyp swims naked towards the shale beach, wades out, white, gleaming. Daly and Mann are dried, half-dressed on the bank, polishing their boots.

DALY: Let's have you, Gyppo. The Scots are comin' ...

Gyp holds his hand up, listening. They listen with him. He smiles.

GYP: Dove. Little bugger.

Trees, side of road. Ellen Pearson, hair gleaming, brushes Billy's coat with handsful of coarse grass; watches Jack Dunn get ready. He slides a neatly folded jacket from his pack, smoothes it onto his wiry body. From the top pocket he takes three war medals; pins them on his lapel, beneath his union badge. Looks at her. Cut to

Edge of the town; church clock striking noon. A line of uniformed police block Westgate. A police inspector stares at the approach of the marching group, establishes it's them, nods to a waiting constable, who pedals his cycle off into the town. A young man, sandy-haired, unshaven, dressed for marching, leans against a wall making notes in a small book, his pack at his feet. The inspector eyes him frostily.

INSPECTOR: *(sotto, to the young man)* I've warned you, if there's trouble, I won't be responsible for your safety.

The young man nods, continues writing. Dunn calls his convoy to a halt twenty feet or so from the police line. Gyp, Daly and Mann break ranks to join him, shoulder to shoulder. Campaign medals gleam on their lapels; boots shine; hair's slicked; Gypsy, medal-less, sports a battered brown derby, his Miners Union badge proud above the brim. March and Union banners flutter on the prow of the cart.

INSPECTOR: *(calling)* Do you have a leader?

Dunn takes a step forward, eyes dark, burning.

INSPECTOR: Is this all you are? *(Dunn nods)* You will please to stay here. A magistrate has been sent for.

The two men stare at each other in silence.

GYP: *(low, angry)* I thought this was a free country, Jack ...

DUNN: *(sotto)* Easy, Gyp. *(to the Inspector)* This is England, mister. Under what law do you prevent our free passage along a public highway about our lawful business?

The inspector ignores the question, gives the order to draw truncheons. Truncheons are drawn. A thin wind blows in from the north; cloud covers sun.

DUNN: *(obdurate)* I repeat: under what law ...?

INSPECTOR: ... A magistrate will be here directly. Just hold your ground, if you know what's good for you ...

The lines of men face each other in silence: truncheons at the port; walking staffs twitching in marchers' hands. The young man with the notebook steps forward into the space between them; approaches the convoy.

YOUNG MAN: *(Ulster clear in the low voice)* Comrade Dunn? *(Jack frowns, not answering)* My name's Phelan, I'm a freelance reporter, covering the northern march for the Herald ... Here, take this.

He hands Dunn the morning's copy. Turns to watch the magistrate's car approach the rear of the police line. Dunn opens the rolled paper. Reads a pencil message on the top: They're looking for trouble. Don't be provoked. Explain later. *Beneath, only glimpsed in the shot, the day's headline: Hitler takes power in Germany.*

The young man winks at Dunn, retires to his wall as the magistrate strides forward, the Inspector at his side.

MAGISTRATE: *(arriving)* Is this all they are?

INSPECTOR: Probably just the advance column, Sir John. We'd been told to expect several dozen ...

MAGISTRATE: *(halting some paces away)* Good God, there's a woman in their midst. Have your men put up truncheons at once. *(The Inspector relays the order. Formal address:)* My name is Sir John Feather, Chairman of Magistrates for this district. Under the powers vested in me by the Public Order Act of 1926 as amended, I must ask you to make known your business in this borough, so that I might determine whether you intend to breach the peace or otherwise disturb the tranquillity of the realm.

DUNN: *(slow, terse)* We're five unemployed men and women looking for work. I had not heard the Public Order Act of 1926 as amended made that a crime. Especially since we've been told for years that we may not claim benefit or assistance unless we can show we have 'genuinely sought work'...

MAGISTRATE: ... My man, I will not bandy words with you, two nights ago a large band of Scottish ruffians attired like yourselves and bearing the same banners caused untold damage to property in this town ... Thirty nine of them are even now in custody awaiting trial ...

on charges ranging from incitement to riot, to wilful assault, drunkenness and sundry other breaches of the peace ... I will know your purpose here ...

DUNN: *(quick, louder, still controlled)* ... We <u>have</u> no purpose here. We're passing through.

A stand-off, silent, quite intense. The magistrate turns suddenly for words with the Inspector. Dunn catches the young man's eye. The man smiles; raises a clenched fist. Percy Mann coughs suddenly, a spasm he tries to control.

GYP: *(low-voiced chuckle)* Sounds like your countrymen made themselves at home, Will ...

DALY: Aye. But they maybe tell a different story.

MAGISTRATE: *(tight-lipped; decided)* Very well. As of now, I am satisfied you represent no threat to the peace of this borough. You may go about your business.

He strides off to his car, through the breaking ranks of the law. Dunn watches a moment, signals On; the convoy trundles forward. The young man collects his pack, follows at a distance.

Slowed mute images of the passage through the town. People applaud from pavements, come forward to press small presents on them for the journey. Gyp has a mouth-organ to his lips. Over, trailed forward, Phelan's voice explaining the fate of the Scots.

PHELAN: *(over)* ... The Government's running scared, it doesn't want this demonstration to succeed and it's organizing a countrywide operation to defeat it. We didn't get wind o' this till we'd arrived here – Andy Mac had a letter poste restante from the National Organizers warning us police informers had infiltrated the march – but I guess it was already too late, the trap was sprung and we were in it. We had sick men, there was snow on the ground, and we'd agreed to wait for your people; so we put down in a farmer's field. The police arrived in strength at midnight, on the dot, and cleared us off the land. So we marched on the workhouse and demanded to be put up in the casual wards. The Master had his speech all ready for us, probably drafted by the Home Office: the casual wards couldn't cope, so he'd have to house us as vagrants, locked up in cells at night and all the rest of it. The men refused point-blank, marched to an empty casual ward, took possession. Within minutes the police were back – they must've bin waiting at the gates for the call – and waded into us with truncheons … It was quite an operation …

Afternoon. A great oak, at the heart of a vast meadow. The group sit in a rough circle beneath the tree, eating their rations and dealing with personal repairs. Jack Dunn sits outside the group but within earshot; works on the map on his knee. Billy frisks around the great field, for the moment freed. Michael Phelan gathers tin plates for the wash-bucket, watches Ellen instruct Gyp in sock-darning. She looks up briefly, catches his gaze, half smiles, looks down again. Percy Mann rubs grass on his blistered feet. Will Daly flicks bleak looks in Dunn's direction; broods.

PHELAN: *(to no-one)* Ye know, I hadn't imagined a woman on the march, begod …

DALY: *(short)* Us neither.

GYP: *(fond)* What d'ye mean, a woman? She's a qualified teacher.

Ellen throws his sock at him, goes to help Percy with his feet.

DALY: So now they're all in clink, is that right?

PHELAN: Aye, that they are …

DALY: All except you, that is.

A silence. Dunn looks across the circle. Phelan goes on with the chore, head down.

DALY: How come?

PHELAN: *(quiet)* Well, as a matter of fact, I was locked up with the rest … They dropped the charges this morning, when they'd checked my bona fides at the Herald …

MANN: Ha. Ah'd allus wondered what they meant by the freedom of the press …

The moment hangs, unresolved. Billy's wandered over, nosing scraps. Daly whacks him over the nose with a stick.

DALY: Get away, ye thievin' bugger …

The pony shies off.

GYP: *(sudden; eyes dark, smoky)* Hey. What ye think ye're doin'?

DALY: I'm gettin' his bloody nose outa my plate.

GYP: ... Well don't. Ye think cloutin' 'im's gonna stop 'im bein' hungry ...?

DALY: ... He's a <u>field</u> o' food here, man ...

GYP: ... He's lived wi' folk all 'is life, he's used to sharin' ... And he's doin' his job, like you an' me ... Show some respect ...

DALY: He's a <u>horse,</u> for chrissake.

GYP: *(implacable)* No matter.

Daly gets up, not happy; throws the stick at the oak. Dunn moves slowly in, map and notebook in hand, ignoring the spat.

DUNN: Right. I've worked out a new route ... It's a bit further but a sight safer, I reckon. Look in.

He lays the map in the circle of feet, a stick for the pencil line.

DALY: Hold on a minute, Jack. What about our comrades back there ...?

DUNN: *(calm)* I've told you already, Will ... there's nothing to be done about that ...

DALY: ... We could go back an' try an' see 'em ... Arrange a lawyer frae the union for 'em ...

DUNN: *(patient, deliberate)* ... Will, I've already said, we'll inform the March Organizers as soon as we ...

PHELAN: *(quiet)* No need. S'done. I called the Herald this morning, they said they'd let Wal Hannington know in person ...

They look at him.

DUNN: *(slow)* Good work. *(Pause. Daly begins again)* <u>No</u>, Will. There's nothing we can <u>do</u> back there. 'Cept maybe end up inside with 'em. We've got to get on.

He traces out the new route with the stick. Sound fades. Trail Dunn's journal voice and mix to a montage sequence, sometimes mute, iconized, sometimes voiced, of their progress west and south into Lancashire. Versions of Pit Lie Idle-o, *coming and going, bind the sequence of scenes and images. As previously, two time-codes are in play: theirs (about a fortnight); ours (around four years).*

DUNN: *(Journal voice over)* ... The fate of the Scots boys at Tow Law and the clear preparation the police had been able to make for our arrivals have caused us to shift ground. We hope all sections will have had the news in time to reroute their journey down ... With luck, we'll

reach Lancashire in time to join up with the North-West contingent …
But it'll mean a longer spell of roughing it than we'd hoped for, no
'safe houses' to bunk down in for a while, and no wider company of
comrades to ease the frictions of the journey … The young Irishman
comes with us, hungry for stories, and helps take our minds off old
Percy's chest and feet, Will's persistent ill-humour, Ellen's grieving
silences and a spring as fickle and full of false promises as a British
Labour Party in office …

Day. Mute. They climb a hill-road, heads down against a driving wind.

*Evening. Mute. Steady soaking rain. They march towards and past
camera, sodden, worn, a touch dispirited. Ahead, edge of frame, a
church on high ground.*

*Night. Methodist hill-church, small, clean, very bare, dimly lit at one end
by miners' lamps. The original five sleep exhausted on separate benches
at the back of the church. In a small adjoining room, door open, Michael
Phelan stands in his longjohns drying their clothes before a meagre fire.
Dunn's folded maps fall from his jacket pocket, Phelan picks them up, his
finger traces the pencil line to the edge of Manchester. The second map.
He draws his lamp closer; studies the pencilled journey.*

*Early morning. On the march again, past fields hard with frost, snow on
the air, faces rawn with wind. Gyp chats with Billy in the rear.*

GYP: … Aye, aye, I know what ye're thinkin', bonnie lad, but ye see …
   the problem wi' Spring is … it's like the struggle, see … for every
   step ye take forwards, ye'll maybe have to take a couple back …

*Will Daly drops back to share Billy's bridle; feeds him a crust. The two
men share a look.*

*Night. They've made camp in a clearing in a thick copse of trees. The six
sit talking, shrouded in their blankets, around the fire they've built.
Phelan makes notes in his book; Dunn's writing a letter to his wife:
elements of each asynchronously collated, make up the scene.*

MANN: … 1872 or 3, ah think … ah were twelve at the time … aye, that
   was the first time ah was iver on strike, the owners'd sacked a whole
   shift fer refusin' to work chest deep in water … The good old days …
   So they closed t'pits 'n tried t' starve us back, just like now … put
   their names around the area … 'the politicians' they wor known as …
   activists … couldn't get a job nowhere, many a time they couldn't get
   benefit'r poor relief either … S'allus been the same …

Dunn's letter begins.

DUNN: *(over)* Dear Mary, if things go well I expect to be passing through Leighley around the 27th, with a band of unemployed comrades on our way to join the great march on London. I'd be … glad if you would have a word with your dad and see if the Trades Council could put us up for a day or two. There's six of us, one a woman …

ELLEN: … My mam worked in Stoke growing up. Pot painter. This is one of hers … *(She holds the tea mug she drinks from to the light. Flamed faces study it: perhaps a Clarice Cliff, simple, elegant, understated)* I had it for a wedding present. There's nothing I own more beautiful … People's art. It's everywhere. And it's invisible …

Phelan stares up at her across the fire, pencil arrested above the pad, eyes alive.

DUNN: *(Letter, over)* … It'll be good to see the boy and let him know I love and care about him. You too, love, if you have the time and a wish to … I've missed you keen, Mary, missed having you in my life, I suppose … But I'll respect the new life you're making there, whatever that is …

He stops, looks over at Gyp, who's begun tuning his mouth-organ.

GYP: … This one ah call A Hewer's Dream. *(He sings)*
    Ah'm a hewer of coal
    Under someone else's land
    And why he should own it
    Ah'll niver understand
    Now a hewer's no brains
    As all wise folk know
    But a hewer can dream
    From the dark down below
    And I dreamed I was flying, as free as the air
    In the sky above Durham, my county so fair
    And below I heard weeping and screaming and pain
    And I looked for its cause and saw profit and gain.

Phelan holds his hand out for the mouth-organ, feels his way into the accompaniment.

    And further afield
    In the cities and towns
    Ah saw fear, ah smelt hunger

Ah heard terrible sounds
And all across England,
Across Scotland and Wales,
There lay wealth beyond counting
Weighing justice's scales
And as I dreamed I was flying, free as the air,
In the sky above England, my country so fair,
Came a cry slowly lifting, full of purpose and power:
Though our blood run in rivers, we will take this no more.
And O they joined in a union of bodies and minds,
They marched on the future, the past left behind;
And the battle was quick, the battle was fair,
But the old world was broken, and a new one was there.

Phelan lets the mouth-organ rest. Gyp finishes unaccompanied.

Now a hewer's no brains
As all wise folk know
But a hewer can dream
From the dark down below.

Early morning. Michael Phelan phones London from a kiosk, dictating copy from his notebook. Ahead, through the glass, Will Daly carries rations in a cardboard box from a village grocery, lifts it up to Gyp on the back of the cart.

Morning. Dales turning to Pennines, miles from anywhere. Low bleak sky. Slow tracking shot of the six, backs to camera, staring through a wire mesh perimeter fence. We see a newly painted notice board: Ministry of Labour – Pennine Training Camp. Beyond, wooden huts around a tarmac square, on which a couple of dozen thin-faced uniformed workers (navy blue serge blouses, jackets, berets, boots), at the salute, sing God Save the King *as the Union Jack's run up the flagpole.*

Over this, an unfolding caption:
'After all, sound nutrition in a pregnant woman is obviously the only way of sustaining her health and strength and that of her forthcoming child. She should become accustomed to a diet that includes ample milk – two pints a day – cheese, butter, eggs, fish, liver, fruit, and fresh vegetables, which will supply her body with the essential elements, salts and vitamins.'

Sir George Newman, Chief Medical Officer, Ministry of Health. Report on High Maternal Mortality Rate, 1932.

The men port shovels and are marched to the stone-breaking site by the training instructor. Trail sounds of retching.

Ellen Pearson stands by a shallow stream, retching and kecking. Phelan watches her from the top of a sloping bank. A bucket of dirty plates and mugs lies at her feet.

PHELAN: Are you ill, Ellen?

ELLEN: *(seeing him)* No. I'm all right.

He joins her. Eases her onto a large block of limestone on the bank. Begins washing pots and tin plates. Ellen dries her mouth; watches him.

ELLEN: Where are you from?

PHELAN: Donegal. Belfast. Fife. Oxford.

ELLEN: Oxford?

PHELAN: I'm a student. Ruskin College. Doing this for my thesis. The Herald're helping out.*(Silence. He looks up at her. She looks away. He washes on. From nowhere)* How did he die? Your husband?

ELLEN: *(eventually)* He drowned.

PHELAN: What, on the boats?

ELLEN: No. In a reservoir.

PHELAN: Ah. *(Thinks)* Swimming, you mean?

ELLEN: No. *(Silence)* He couldn't swim.

She gets up, climbs the bank, heads for the others by the road. Phelan buckets the pots; follows her.

Day. Slow hovering track in through thick mist. A church bell tolls, miles off; closer, disconnected shouts, dying in the dense air. The cart's revealed, tilted and buckled, in a steep ditch; dim figures try to right it. Ellen Pearson kneels by Billy's head, soothing him as he struggles to free himself. Percy Mann wheezes and splutters in the damp.

Half an hour's elapsed. The cart's out and righted. Gyp examines a wheel; it's buckled, the metal rim sprung from the wood. Ellen walks Billy, calming him. The church bell stops. Close shot Jack Dunn, listening. Frail disembodied sounds, closing; calls bending in the dankness. Dark shapes slowly loom from nothing: cows; two gaunt men;

a lad; a dewsodden collie, flat to the road, holding the cows, some yards from the group, unbidden. They stand. Silence.

DUNN: *(eventually)* Good-day. We had an accident. *(Points to the cart)* Wheel's gone.

The shorter of the two cowmen slowly approaches; examines the fractured wheel in silence; begins to read the march placards on the side of the cart.

COWMAN: This you people?

DUNN: Aye.

The man nods. Looks back at the wheel.

COWMAN: Tek a good two hours, will that.

DUNN: *(carefully)* Listen. We're skint …

The man gives him a thin smile.

COWMAN: Ah thowt thee might be. *(Calling)* Martin. *(The kid, 15, looms)* Run tell thi mother we've company fer t'pot. *(The lad's gone)* Ah've these to field an' then ah'm done. Easter Sunday. Half day. Watch thi backs …

Two short whistles. The dog has the cows on the move, looming and fading past the watching group.

The mist has receded; a mid-afternoon April sun warms the bleak countryside. Loose shot of a gathering of people seated at trestle tables before a pair of meagre tied cottages. Billy grazes, on tether; the cart's fixed. Church bells again, closer.

Shot of the tables, being laid for a meal by the older children from both houses. The second cowman's wife appears, jugs of root beer in her hands, fills mugs and cups down the table. Dunn and the rest sit in the midst of cowmen and young; when the servers are seated, there'll be nine kids, ten grown-ups. Phelan entertains a group of infants with coin-tricks. Ellen watches him across the table. Jack Dunn raises his glass to the hosts.

DUNN: Thank you.

COWMAN: *(returning it)* Your health.

The two wives arrive from the house, large pots in their hands, Martin and others behind them with home-baked soda bread. The first cowman's wife lays her pot before her husband, for serving.

COWMAN'S WIFE: *(to table)* It's not much. But you're welcome.

She goes to sit down. The cowman joins his hands, the kids follow suit.

COWMAN: We'll pray.

WIFE: Wait on, I've left someat inside ...

She leaves, returns with two jugs of spring flowers, lays one at each end of the table, resumes her seat, head on hands for the prayer.

COWMAN: *(quiet, distinct)* Lord. Another day wi' someat on our plates.
   We thank thi. And ask thi t'heed the prayers o' them wi' less. Amen.

He lifts the pot-lid, digs his serving spoon into the stew, raises a rabbit's carcase on it to the table.

COWMAN: Say 'ello to the Easter Bunny ...

Kids squeak with laughter. Men and women smile.

Early evening. Cowman's cottage. Kitchen-living space, cramped, mean. Gyp does dishes at the sink. Phelan carries steaming mugs of tea to the two women, feet up by the stove. Voices from above: Ellen's, kids'. Daly calls from outside by the cart: two minutes. Phelan winks at Gyp, takes the bare narrow stairs to the bedspaces.

Billy's back in the shafts. The cowman studies the mended wheel with his hands. Dunn watches him. Daly repacks gear on the cart above them.

COWMAN: *(standing)* Aye, that s'd hold. Ah'd like t'offer thee a bed, but
   as tha can see ...

DUNN: Nay, you've done us proud. And we thank you ...

DALY: We do that ...

The cowman sniffs, walks Dunn slowly towards the gate, eyes checking weather as he goes.

COWMAN: Be cowd t'neet ... the Owner's an owd barn on th'edge o'
   th'estate 'e dunt use, it's on thi way ...

They stop by the gate. Stare at the bleak sky ahead.

DUNN: What's he pay, this Owner o'yours?

COWMAN: Twenty seven bob a week. *(indicates the hovel)* Less four
   an'nine fer that ...

DUNN: And what's a week round these parts?

COWMAN: Fifty four hours. Four days holiday a year.

DUNN: *(weighing it; quiet)* You need a union, brother.

COWMAN: *(simple)* Oh there's a union. Me an' Eddie sent fer forms a year
sin'. But we get our mails through t'Big House … he opened t'buggers.
Telled us we'd be out on our necks, kids 'n all, t'day we joined …

Dunn sniffs. They stare at the skyline together. Trail Ellen's voice.

*Cottage. Upstairs. Phelan in doorway, watching. Reverse to Ellen sitting
on a large mattress in a corner, five bed-ready nippers around her,
reading from a book.*

ELLEN:
'… He smiled as he heard the jeers, and there was a shake of the hand,
He spoke like a friend long known; and lo! I was one of the band.
And now the streets seem gay and the high stars glittering bright;
And for me, I sing amongst them, for my heart is full and light.
I see the deeds to be done and the day to come on the earth,
And riches vanished away and sorrow turned to mirth;
I see the city squalor and the country stupour gone.
And we a part of it all – we twain no longer alone
In the days to come of the pleasure, in the days that are of the fight –
I was born once long ago: I am born again tonight.'

*She closes the book. Sees Phelan in the doorway. He's moved. The kids
want more.*

PHELAN: *(gently)* March time.

*She smiles palely. Gives the book to the eldest child. Kisses each in turn.
Leaves. The kids scutter to the foot-square window to watch the
departure. The book rests on the bed. Slow track in to collect the title:
Selected Poems: William Morris.*

*Night. Disused barn, edge of the estate. Low light from within flickers
through holes in the structure.*

Dunn's voice over track in: quiet, distinct, serious:

'… As long as I breathe I shall fight for the future, that radiant future,
in which man, strong and beautiful, will become master of the drifting
stream of his own history …'

*Barn. Mann, Daly and Gyp sleep in their blankets. Dunn and Phelan,
scoops of light in the dark, are still up. Billy champs on hay in a far*

corner. Dunn closes the book on his lap, organizes his blanket for sleep. Phelan thinks; watches him.

PHELAN: What's that?

DUNN: 'On Optimism and Pessimism'. 1901. Trotsky.

PHELAN: *(low)* When will you go? *(Dunn looks, frowns)* Russia. I saw the map…

DUNN: *(smiles)* Just a dream.

PHELAN: I have it too.

Silence. Dunn notes Ellen's empty bed-space.

DUNN: Is she all right?

PHELAN: I think maybe she's sickening … I'll see she's OK. May I borrow that …?

Dunn hands him the Trotsky essays; settles for sleep. Phelan flicks the pages; reads. Mix to

Night. Mute. Shots through glass of the Owner's Big House: a dinner party, twelve at table, candelabra, silver, beef, claret, cut glass; service, order; kitchens, a seethe of sweat and steam; a nursery, three young girls in party dress listening to a Superhet cabinet model wireless; billiard room, electric light over empty green baize; others.

Shots of Ellen's face, reading the lives.

Night. Ellen follows a narrow path through trees back towards the barn; stops; lifts her lamp; sees Phelan ahead, staring at her. He approaches slowly; stands close. Eyes meet in the silence. His hands move up to her head, begin to remove her funeral headband; she makes to stop him: all as if in slow motion. The headband's off, the hair freed, swaying. His mouth closes on hers. The kiss holds, grows for some moments, then she tries to resist his pressure. Words invade the kiss without ending it.

ELLEN: No …

PHELAN: Why …?

ELLEN: No no …

PHELAN: I want you. Want me …

ELLEN: Please Michael …

PHELAN: Is it that? *(headband)* You've grieved enough, woman …

ELLEN: … Not that …

PHELAN: What, what …?

ELLEN: … I'm carrying his child … *(The kiss cools, slows. Faces detach. Eyes focus)* I think I'm carrying his child …

PHELAN: Why should it matter … If I want you … And you want me …?

ELLEN: *(tears stinging eyes)* It might have mattered to <u>him</u>, Michael. If he'd known. Perhaps he wouldn't have done what he did.

Phelan draws her to him, rests his face in her hair, moved and bewildered.

PHELAN: Oh love. Oh lovely love.

Morning. The six stand on the crest of a Pennine ridge, looking south towards the Lancashire conurbations. The image holds only briefly, gives way to

Mute. Actuality footage of Lancashire urban life and conditions of mid-thirties: work, dole, social life, struggle; smoke, grime, poverty, rickets, decay; hovels, evictions; the sequence cut precisely to the massive strains of the English Anthem 'Land of Hope and Glory'. Threading through, there but not dominant, the march goes on, past Daily Herald and other hoardings and posters recording the doings of the larger world: Hitler, Mussolini, Franco – the Civil War in Spain.

Long shot, terraced row of pit cottages, Leighley, between Wigan and Manchester. Phelan minds horse and cart outside one of the houses. Kids surround them.

Pit cottage, front room, Sunday's room, neat, calm, ordered behind net curtains. Jack Dunn stands in it, reading its signs. Photographs line the mantelpiece: he traces the lines of growth in his wife, from child to bride. Around the walls, union emblems and certificates; framed mementoes of family lost in wars; on a sideboard, two fishing trophies and a copper bust of Marx. From the kitchen, the low murmur, occasional laughter, of the others. He returns his gaze to the mantelpiece, the framed shot of his wedding we've seen back in Durham.

MAN (AARON): *(arriving from kitchen,)* … There's a note there fer thi, behind t'clock … She's found a place i' Gorman Street, it's not far …

Dunn smiles, nods, takes the envelope down, joins his father-in-law at the table. The old miner opens a small cash-box, counts out six pounds and a few coppers onto the mahogany. Hands him a book and pencil.

AARON: Here, sign for this.

DUNN: *(signing)* What is it?

AARON: Five pounds from union funds, one pound two and seven from a raffle we ran at the Club ...

Dunn thanks him, puts the coins into a cloth moneybag in his coat pocket.

DUNN: What was the prize, Arthur?

AARON: A trip to Madrid, all expenses paid.

Dunn nods, sombre suddenly.

AARON: T'vicar had t'winning ticket. *(He grins. Dunn too, after a moment)* In the best traditions of the Church, he's redonated it ... Draw's toneet ... *(Hands Dunn a sheet of paper)* Right, here's your addresses, they'll feed and succour ye for as long as you're stoppin' ... There's a bed 'ere for thee ...

Dunn looks down at the unopened envelope in his hands. Gypsy's voice lifts suddenly in the kitchen: laughter, rising, receding.

DUNN: Any idea if the Lancashire contingent's set off yet, Arthur?

AARON: Our lot set off Wednesday, they're gathering Stockport or somewhere, I believe ... *(Pause)* What there <u>was</u> of 'em ... The war agin fascism i' Spain's tekin' priority in these parts just now ... *(Sniffs)* If I thowt they'd tek me, I'd bloody go mysen ...

DUNN: *(slowly)* Aye. I know what you mean.

He stands, stares through the window at Phelan, pony, kids.

AARON: I put th'address o' t'Club on that paper ... Be there for eight, will you, it's unemployed neet ...

DUNN: *(not turning)* Right.

Aaron collects his things, prepares to return to the kitchen.

AARON: I'm ... sorry about you and Mary, Jack.

DUNN: Aye.

AARON: She's been a strong 'un all 'er life, right from a child ...

DUNN: *(turns, smiles)* S'all right, Aaron. I'm not here to cause trouble.

His father-in-law leaves. Dunn returns his eyes to the window. The light's faded outside; now the glass begins to give back his own image, framed in the room. Sounds drain away. The window clears. Through it, he sees Phelan being held in conversation by a hard-looking man in a blue suit astride a motor-cycle. The man talks, Phelan takes something down in his black notebook. Dunn frowns, uneasy. Cut to

Night. Miners' Hall. A tater-pie supper in progress: a top table holds Lodge and Area committee members and the marchers; two longer ones run down from it, filled with jobless miners and their wives; a fourth, adjacent but detached, is packed with kids. Pit-boys carry jugs of mild beer from the bar area. Behind the committee's table, the banners of Durham and Lancashire miners are displayed. In a corner, a fiddler tunes up by the piano; a man assembles a drum kit nearby. Jack Dunn checks out the two empty places beside him, looks at Daly, who's buying a penny raffle ticket for Madrid from a prowling pit-boy. Daly shrugs ignorance, mid-process.

Gyp in from the street. He hurries through the throng to a place next to Dunn. He's bathed, spruced, ready for a night.

GYP: *(reaching for food)* … That bloody horse, bugger wouldn't settle, he's not mad on towns … Eh, is that beer? *(He smiles greetings at Phelan and Ellen, pours himself a mug.)* Oh boy.

DUNN: Where's Percy, Gyp?

GYP: *(feeding)* Turned in. Said 'e wanted an early night …

DUNN: *(brooding)* He coulda let me know … Is he all right?

Gyp looks at him steadily for a moment.

GYP: *(simply)* He's tired, Jack.

Dunn nods, looks away, taking but not liking the gentle reproof.

AARON: *(A place away, leaning to whisper)* There'll be a bit of a do after, Jack … They draw t'raffle at ten … A few of us'll be retiring to the Soviet over there for a chat. *(He indicates the committee room)* If you've a mind, you'd be welcome to join us …

Dunn nods. Aaron withdraws.

GYP: *(pouring more mild)* Eh. *(He surveys the scene)* This is grand, what?

Miners' Hall, later. The meal's gone, the room reworked for dance and entertainment. Slow scan of the proceedings: the man with the fiddle's

*up, doing impressions – George Formby, Frank Randle – between tunes.
People sit at filled tables: drink, talk, fun. Gyp's well away, playing
bones by the bar. Daly's deep in talk with a group of young miners.
Phelan and Ellen sit at the same table, not together. Phelan makes notes
for an article in his book. The scan ends on the Committee Room door,
the cardboard sign on it: Meeting in Progress.*

*Committee Room, smoke-filled, lit only over the table that halves the
room. Eight men, Dunn and Aaron among them, sit round it, talking.
Dimly, around them, the walls tell their story: banners, emblems,
photographs, posters, notices; union life, practice, belief. Over the
fireplace, a socialist-realist painting of Lenin in a miner's helmet.*

DUNN: *(quiet, calm, mid-stream)* ... I don't argue Spain's not important,
that'd be stupid, the march of fascism has to be halted and Spain's the
place to do it ... But there's two fronts to any war. And abandoning
the home front for all-out struggle abroad carries risks none of you
seems interested in facing. *(Pause. He relights his pipe; in control; his
element. In the hall outside, an announcement, some cheers and
applause)* Beyond Spain, comrades, in five years or ten, Money's
going to need another war, possibly against Russia herself ... Imagine
what the British working class're gonna make o' that, if we relinquish
the field now to the leadership of the turncoat Labour Party and the
collaborationist TUC ...

LODGE SECRETARY: ... No one's talkin' about leaving the field, brother ...

DUNN: *(through him)* ... Ah don't agree the marching has 'served its
purpose', brothers. There's a long way to go before we've exposed the
moral, social and productive bankruptcy of capitalism in this country.
It's a battle of minds and hearts we're engaged in: it's one we've got
to win. And we've only just started ...

The door opens, Gyp's head appears.

GYP: Someone 'ere to see you, Jack. *(Gyp's look tells him who)* Eh, Will
Daly won the raffle ... the free trip to Spain. *(Grins at Dunn's frown)*
Come on, bonnie lad, she's waitin' on ye ...

He's gone. Dunn stands; pockets his gear.

DUNN: Excuse me, comrades.

*He leaves for the Hall. Looks around for his visitor. Sees, through a file
of people, his wife in the doorway staring at him. Cut to*

Night. They walk in silence down a tow-path. A thin moon flickers in the dead canal.

MARY: That's the school he's at.

She points to the dark hulk of the 19th century elementary school across the canal, gaunt against the sky, half-barracks, half-penitentiary.

MARY: He had a good report Christmas. Always has his head stuck in a book … *(She looks at him. He smiles)* Anyway …

They fall silent again, the walk slow but measured.

DUNN: You've lost weight.

MARY: A few pound. So have you.

DUNN: Aye. Ah've been doin' a lot o' walkin' …

Silence. They reach the end of a long wall. Vagrants huddle round a towpath fire beneath the bridge.

MARY: It's just up here.

Cut to: Night. Cramped bedroom. The boy sleeps, face lit by a held candle. Close shot of Dunn, staring down at him, candle in hand. The boy stirs, as if to wake; the father watches on.

Night. Scullery, Gorman Street. Mary lights the second gas mantle, lays a kettle of water on the hob to boil, spoons tea into a teapot, removes her coat and scarf, tidies her hair in the window reflection. Behind her, Jack Dunn reaches the bottom of the stairs.

DUNN: Asleep.

MARY: There's tomorrow.

DUNN: Aye.

Silence.

MARY: Come in.

He dwells; takes a chair by the fire; stares at the coal flame. Mary hangs her coat up on a peg, lifts the kettle, mashes tea, settles in a chair on the far side of the table, watches him.

MARY: I had visions of you endin' up hatin' me …

DUNN: *(frowning)* Nay.

MARY: Do you understand? Why I had to?

DUNN: Aye. I think so. *(Taps his head)* Here ah do, anyway.

Their eyes meet. He smiles, modest; looks away.

DUNN: Your dad said y'ad a job …

MARY: I scrub houses for the well-to-do. Not a job exactly …

DUNN: You copin'?

MARY: Aye. *(A silence)* What about you?

DUNN: *(headshake)* Ah'm on every employer's blacklist country-wide. *(Pause)* Union's offered me area organizer, if ah want it.

He thinks; says nothing. She begins pouring tea.

MARY: *(eventually)* If you want it? I thought …

DUNN: Yeah, ah'm not so sure any more. *(He coughs heavily; spits the dark mucus into the fire)* Ah've been thinkin' o' goin' to Russia …

Silence. She finishes the tea preparation. Pushes a mug to his side of the table.

MARY: *(quietly)* Is that what you want?

DUNN: Ah think so. Ah think ah've wanted it a long time. Just 'aven't 'ad the … space to see it.

MARY: Oh. Happen I've done you a good turn then. *(He says nothing)* Are you serious …?

DUNN: *(sudden)* What do you want me to say, love? Ah'm broken? Ah miss ye? Ah canna live wi'out ye? Ah hate ye fer leavin' me high an' dry? Ah canna say those things, they're not true, ah'm in one piece, ah can live wi'out ye, ye've allus 'ad the right to build a life wi'out me, an' the boy's yours more than 'e's mine, you've allus put more into 'im …

He looks back at the flames. She watches the quiet pain work its slow way around his frame.

DUNN: *(low)* Ah <u>do</u> miss ye. However ah've … neglected things, you're a special person … in my life, love. Losin' it's hard.

MARY: *(soft)* I know. For myself, I mean. I never stopped loving you. Not for a minute. *(He glances at her, searching meanings, finds no clear ones)* Dad said you had a woman with you. On the march.

DUNN: Aye. Her husband was downta come, but 'e got depressed wi'
things an' ... killed 'imself ... *(Mary winces)* ... Aye. It 'appens.

MARY: Poor man. Poor woman.

DUNN: She's provin' a good comrade. *(A small smile)* Maybe that's the
future, eh?

Silence. She looks away.

MARY: My dad thinks I'm batty ... You'll never meet a better man than
Jack Dunn, he says ... as if I didn't know it. When I say maybe it's
not a man I need right now, his face goes blank, he hasn't the least
idea what I might mean. *(She sips her tea)* Have you?

DUNN: Sometimes I have. Bur'ah'm a man, like Aaron, an' it's not easy
...

Silence.

MARY: *(gentle)* No more is it for me, love. How long will you stop?

DUNN: Just the night. We've got to push on.

Eyes meet again, fix the contradiction, fail to solve it.

MARY: Don't change, will you. I wouldn't want you ... any other way.

*A slow smile, ironic and admiring, grows between them. He turns away
eventually, prods a smoulder of coal into flame with the poker. She
watches. We watch the two of them for some while; slow mix to*

*Morning. Mute. Long high shot of school playground. Dunn and the boy
talk through iron railings. Over this:*

DUNN'S VOICE: *(reading)* 'When I consider any social system that prevails
in the modern world, I can't, so help me God, see it as anything but a
conspiracy of the rich to advance their own interests under the pretext
of organising society. They think up all manner of tricks and dodges,
first for keeping safe their ill-gotten gains, and then for exploiting the
poor by buying their labour as cheaply as possible. Once the rich have
decided these tricks and dodges shall be recognised by society – which
includes the poor as well as the rich – they acquire the force of law.
Thus an unscrupulous minority is led by its insatiable greed to
monopolise what would have been enough to supply the needs of the
whole population ...'

Cut to closer shot of father and son, voiced.

DUNN: Give us a kiss.

The lad offers his lips, Dunn takes them on his.

DUNN: *(shouldering roll-bag)* Ah'll come again. When this is over.

BOY: *(Durham)* Mam said you were goin' to Russia.

Dunn turns. Looks at him.

DUNN: It's possible. You wanta come?

The lad blinks. Smiles.

BOY: Ah wouldn't mind.

Cut back to long high shot again. Mute. Dunn hands the boy a present through the railings; leaves. They wave. Dunn leaves frame. The kid unwraps the present. Over:

DUNN: *(reading voice)* '... And yet, how much happier even these people would be in Utopia.'

Cut back to the boy, the present: a book. He opens it at the title page: Thomas More – Utopia; *and the pencilled inscription* 'With love, Dad' *beneath. Slow fade to black.*

Black. Over, Dunn's journal voice, in thin wind:

DUNN: *(over)* Two hundred years ago there was next to nothing. Two hundred years from now there'll be nothing again. Meantime, we live our lives ...

Bring up shot of the group, now back to five, on a ridge, staring back at the great plain of industrial Lancashire. In slowed motion, they peel back to the road, the march.

DUNN: *(Journal voice over)* Down to five again. Will Daly's off to Spain. On a penny raffle ticket. This morning we said our goodbyes and wished him safe passage. We'll miss him and hope he'll be spared to see a new world forming ... God knows he's worked for it ...

Close shot, the map of the march. Dunn's pencil follows the route south through Cheshire to the rim of Derbyshire, rings a town a mile or so ahead.

ELLEN: *(voice over)* What do you reckon, a mile?

DUNN: *(voice over)* Someat like that. Manage?

ELLEN: *(voice over)* Surely.

Wide shot of village cricket field, a flaked green hut-pavilion on the edge. Late afternoon, cloud, a hint of rain. Billy's unharnessed, tethered; Gyp and Phelan tend Percy Mann by the cart. Phelan holds the old man by the shoulders as he coughs. Gyp's mashing tea nearby from a primus. Dunn and Ellen approach them.

DUNN: *(checking sky)* … Michael, see if you can get some food going, Ellen's off to see if she can fetch a doctor …

MANN: … Nay, bugger it, Jack …

DUNN: … Save your breath, comrade, it's done …

He begins counting coins out from his canvas bag onto Ellen's palm.

DUNN: Here, take a bus if there is one …

PHELAN: Jack, could I have a word?

DUNN: What is it, Michael?

Phelan leaves Percy with Gyp, joins the couple some paces from the cart.

PHELAN: Why don't I go in with Ellen …? I have to call the Herald today and Percy needs something warm inside him, I'm sure he does … I could get it while I'm there …

Dunn considers it. Phelan looks at Ellen, who looks away. Dunn counts more coins out, hands them to Phelan.

DUNN: Soup. And a bit o' brandy. Quick as you can …

He watches the pair hurry off for the gate, the road. Turns to join the others. Percy's in spasm again, neckerchief to mouth. Dunn kneels by the cart-wheel to help Gypsy brace him. The coughing subsides, the yellow cloth comes away from the mouth as he sucks for air. Filmy blood on teeth, lips, neckerchief.

MANN: Ah'll be all right.

DUNN: You'll be fine, Percy. *(A look at the sky; another at Gyp)* See if there's a way into that place, will ye, Gyp, without breakin' anything …

Gyp nods, heads off for the hut. Percy rests, eyes closed, face mottled. Dunn draws the blanket over the frail frame. Cut to

Late afternoon. Country town doctor's waiting room, empty save for Ellen Pearson. She stands reading a wall of Ministry of Health and local notices: infectious illnesses, prescribed nutritional requirements for expectant mothers, fees for consultations and home visits, church fêtes, gymkhanas, women's sewing circles; catches her reflection in a glass panel; decides to remove the mourning band from her hair. A phone rings in the next room; a woman answers, low efficient tones.

High Street store. Phelan packs provisions into a cardboard box as the grocer rehearses the list of purchases and tots up on his pad: cocoa, tea, soup, sliced brawn, bread, peas, aspirin, a half bottle of brandy ...

GROCER: ... Elevenpence ha'penny, one and three the brawn, brandy's seven and two, aspirin's fivepence, fivepence ha'penny the peas ... cocoa, cocoa ... *(Phelan has the stuff packed, waits)* Right, that'll be eleven shillings and sevenpence all together please ...

Phelan lays five half-crowns on the counter.

PHELAN: Eleven and a penny ...

GROCER: *(checking again)* ... Bless my soul, eleven and a penny it is, I'm terribly sorry ...

PHELAN: Mistakes will happen ...

The grocer carries the cash to the till, rings up.

PHELAN: Is there a telephone next door?

GROCER: I believe there is ... Calling home, are you?

PHELAN: Mm.

Doctor's waiting room. Ellen Pearson sits, stares at the opaque glass panel door to the surgery. Silence. A woman's voice, a ting as a receiver's lowered, a chair scrape, the door opens, the doctor's secretary appears.

SECRETARY: ... That was Doctor Balchin returning my call, he's just arrived home ... He says he's afraid there's nothing he can do this evening, if you'd care to bring the patient in tomorrow morning, he'd be happy to see him in surgery ...

ELLEN: ... Did you explain his condition? Did you tell him he was coughing blood ...?

SECRETARY: *(pleasant, implacable)* ... Otherwise, you could try Dr Fry down the High Street, or there's the hospital ...

ELLEN: *(abrupt, on her way)* Thank you.

SECRETARY: Let me give you the address of the hospital.

Ellen finds her control, waits, lets the woman find the card; takes it. Close shot of her face as she reads it.

SECRETARY: *(voice over)* The master's a sensible soul. Once he's been signed in, there should be no problems ...

Close shot of the card: Meanwood Workhouse and Hospital for the Poor *and an address. Over, telephone operator's voice: 'Yes, the charge has been accepted, you may go ahead ...' Cut to*

High Street inn. Largeish best room, early evening, just opened. Phelan, phone to ear, at a corner of the bar.

PHELAN: Hello, give me extension three seven, will ya ...

He watches the publican clean a pump handle, stare morosely at the empty room, glance at him.

PHELAN: It's all right. They're paying ...

The publican nods, leaves to serve an old man just entered the snug. Phelan swings back to the call again, connected.

PHELAN: *(low-voiced)* It's Phelan ... *(He listens at once, jaw set, frame tensed. Eventually)* No, now just a minute, mister ...

He falls abruptly quiet, silenced.

Best room. Shot of Phelan, back to entrance, still at the phone, speaking in low tones. Behind him, down the long room, Ellen hovers in the doorway, gradually makes a slow advance into the room to catch Phelan's eye.

PHELAN: *(front of shot, face tense)* ... Look, mister, let me tell you something ... *(lifts as the man interrupts)* No, you listen to <u>me</u> for a change ... This is dirty work, do you understand? Dirty and shaming. An' I've done it for you, God help me, for one reason and one reason only, an' I wanna know what's happenin' wi' my da', you promised he'd be out by now ...

The man at the other end begins to prevaricate. Phelan listens. In the back of the shot, the publican appears frowningly from the snug, approaches the listening pale-faced Ellen.

PHELAN: *(firing in)* ... What do you mean, you're not sure you can do anything now? ... You lay so much as finger on him, after what ye have me doin' for ye, I'll do for ye, so I will ...

The publican greets Ellen, Phelan spins, sees her, the receiver talking on in his hand as the look holds.

PUBLICAN: *(peremptory; already committed)* ... No unaccompanied ladies in this establishment, petal. Rule of the house.

Phelan houses the receiver, cutting the call mid-argument. Neither looks at the publican, each deep in the search for meaning.

ELLEN: *(impassive)* Are you finished?

Phelan nods, gathers the provision box; strides past her for the door and out.

PUBLICAN: ... I hope you'll excuse me, ma'am, I 'ad no idea you were together ...

ELLEN: *(slowly)* You ... ignorant man.

She leaves by the glass and oak doors; they swing stutteringly behind her.

Evening. High Street, pavement. Phelan watches her emerge from the inn, approach, stop some paces away. Neither speaks for some moments, the phone call between them. Something has disturbed her; he sees it.

ELLEN: Take the food back, will you? Tell Jack I can't get a doctor out, I'm going to find the hospital ...

PHELAN: ... Let me do that ...

ELLEN: I'll do it. *(Pause)* Go on.

PHELAN: Ellen ... In there ...

ELLEN: Michael. *(He stops; pleads for her help)* Tell me when you know what you need to say. *(He nods, slow, pale in the gloom)* I know you're in trouble. *(Silence)* Come here. *(She takes him in her arms, gently, like a mother)* Trust me.

Phelan's eyes are big with tears. He pulls away from her, fights them; stares at her half-fiercely, as if at bay; swings abruptly away and off into the dusk. Close shot of Ellen watching him, love and unease at work in the face.

Evening, around eight. Shot of hut-pavilion, a pair of window-shutters expertly unhinged to give entry. Over, Percy Mann's voice, interior acoustic.

MANN: *(over; a fever-ramble)* ... You know wor 'e said, my dad, straight out to 'is face, ah wa' there, a pit-boy by 'is side ...

A coughing spasm.

Pavilion. Dark close shot of Dunn cool-sponging Mann's upper body at one end of the space. At the other, Gyp cleans and fills the miners' lamps for the night.

MANN: *(recovering)* ... 'E said, Ye might be Lord Gowrie and ownera this coalmine but ye've only one arse to shit through like everyone else an' the trouble wi' thine is it sits right over wor bloody heads ... *(He cackles, coughs again)* ... Jack, Jack boy ...

DUNN: Here, Percy ... *(He leans in)* How you feel?

MANN: Don't send me back.

DUNN: *(slow)* Sleep, eh?

MANN: Aye.

Mann rests, eyes closed. Dunn dabs the frail face with the cloth.

GYP: She's 'ere, Jack ...

Dunn nods. Draws the blanket over the sick man. Leaves the cricket-pad bed to join Ellen by the window. Gyp crouches by the primus, warming her soup.

ELLEN: How is he?

DUNN: Not good. You find the hospital?

ELLEN: *(nods)* Here ... I drew a map on the other side ...

She hands him the hospital card, sits on a box to eat her food. Dunn studies the card, turns it over; hands it to Gyp, who reads it, hands it back.

GYP: *(simply)* 'E'll not go in one o' them places awake, I can tell ye ...

DUNN: He needs looking at. If it's a chill, we'll wait ... Worse an' we'll have to send him home.

Long silence. Gyp hands Ellen her soup, crosses to stand by the darkening window.

DUNN: *(undeflected)* That has to be correct, Gyp.

GYP: *(soft; bitter)* Aye. Maybe. Has to be more than correct, Jack. Has to be right.

Silence. It hovers.

MANN: *(over; clear; dream-talk)* ... Ah loved it Fridays love when yer 'ands wor slick wi' goose-grease from doin' my back ...

Silence. Gyp looks at Dunn, crosses to Mann's pallet up the hut, squats to tend him. Dunn takes his place at the window, stares out at the dark field. Billy walks round the tilted cart, hobbled. Ellen eats her soup and bread, watching him in quarter profile.

DUNN: *(not turning)* What's wrong with Michael? Do you know?

Ellen sets down her tin bowl, uneasy, uncertain. Dunn turns to look at her.

ELLEN: I don't know. Why, what happened?

DUNN: He came back looking like a ghost, went out again, last we've seen of him. *(She pours a mug of tea, eyes averted)* Ah don't pry, Ellen. But if there's a problem, ah need to know.

Silence. Up the room, Gyp coaxes Percy with the brandy.

ELLEN: *(carefully)* I can't say if there's a problem or not ... But if there is, you'll hear about it. Will that suit?

They look at each other levelly across the tight dark space for a moment.

DUNN: Aye. Ah suppose.

He turns away to the window again. Sees Michael Phelan stroking Billy's ears. A church clock strikes: eight. Gyp returns from the bed area; stands, brooding.

GYP: What's the decision then?

DUNN: Sort the cart out, will you, Gyp? Michael can help ... We'll take him in, get him looked at, decide what to do when we know what we're facing. *(Looks at Gyp)* All right?

GYP: *(slow)* Aye.

Dunn moves from the window, Gyp eases his big frame through it, heads for the cart. Dunn begins packing gear into Percy's haversack. Ellen sips her tea, watching him. Dunn returns, begins packing his roll-bag.

DUNN: *(quiet)* One of us'll have to spend the night with Perce. Will you be ... all right for an hour or so?

ELLEN: I'll be fine. *(she watches him prepare two lamps for lighting)* What's bothering Gyp?

DUNN: He thinks I'm going to send Perce home.

ELLEN: Are you?

DUNN: If I have to.

ELLEN: The man could die ... I don't understand ...

DUNN: We did the first march together, Gyp and me. Winter of 1922. Percy was section leader, fourteen of us all told, a cold time we had of it. Half way down, a coupla the older lads got sick, Percy told 'em they'd have to go home. The lads refused; said they'd sooner die in their boots doin' someat useful than in a chair starin' at the fire ... Next night it went fourteen below, froze the field we slept in. The old fellers went back in mail-bags. Somea the boys thought Percy shoulda made 'em. Percy made a speech over the bodies at Nottingham Central. He said: Those comrades had paid their dues. I do not argue I did right. I simply say they'd earned the right to choose. *(Long pause, as he confronts the final meaning)* We honour them. They show us there is pride in dying.

The lamps are lit. Creak of the cart as it's backed towards the verandah. Michael Phelan appears at the window; gazes at Ellen for a moment. Dunn hands him two lamps and bags, he recedes into the gloom.

MANN: *(over, a croak)* ... I'm all crazy, just for the love of you ...

Cut to slow, looming track of nineteenth century workhouse buildings in moonlight, over roadway wall. A church clock strikes nine.

GYP: *(voice over; interior acoustic)* Dinna worrit, Perce, ah have ye safe ...

Track ends on a shot of the institutional façaded entrance, Billy and cart untended by the steps. Cut to

Workhouse entrance hall, dimly lit. Gyp stands some paces in, the blanketed Percy in his arms like laundry. Some way away, Dunn watches an under-manager processing the sick man's documents of entitlement behind a closed window partition. A wall-clock wheezes, on the lip of striking the half.

GYP: *(soft)* 'E's boilin' up again.

Dunn turns, nods. The under-manager stamps documents and admission forms, clips them together, slides the window open, lays the papers on the counter.

UNDER-MANAGER: Wait here.

The man leaves his stool, enters the hall, heads off down a corridor, knocks respectfully at a door, enters. Silence.

Close shot Dunn; Gyp; Mann, eyes closed. Off their faces, an imaged sequence essentializes the workhouse and its relationship to their class: cheese and bread being meticulously sliced, weighed, plated on a kitchen counter; the 'casual wards', vagrants' cells and attached work-holes; the dining room overseen by huge framed pictures of ruling-class dignitaries; drilled corridors.

A door clicks. Footsteps. The under-manager's returned to his stool, a mound of paper still to process. Dunn waits a moment, ignored.

DUNN: *(quietly)* Are we finished ...?

UNDER-MANAGER: Wait there ... Transfers need the Master's approval ... The Master's busy just now.

DUNN: *(slowly)* Did you tell him we have a sick man here ...?

UNDER-MANAGER: ... I told you he's busy. And he doesn't like caps indoors ...

Dunn absorbs this a moment; looks at Gyp, eyes bright in the dark light. Cut to

Office. The master eats at his desk, pours ale carefully from an enamel jug, reads a copy of the Daily Mail propped amidst his cold plate supper. Shot of the article he reads: a sympathetic examination of Mosley and the Nazi solution to Britain's social ills. A clatter of sound in the corridor disturbs him; the door swings open, Dunn appears, Gyp and the sick Mann behind him, the Under-Manager in their wake.

MASTER: *(half-rising)* What the devil do you think you're ...

DUNN: *(fast; terse)* ... Sit down, don't speak, don't move ... *(Places admission forms before him)* ... Now, do your duty and sign those, if you would, and we can get this poor man to a doctor ...

MASTER: *(reaching for telephone)* ... You can't speak to me like this, I'll have you ...

DUNN: *(there first; distinct)* Gyp.

Gyp advances to the desk, shows him the sick man. The Master takes him in palely. In the silence, Percy's eyes open, take in the room, the Master.

MANN: *(a faint creak)* Bastard.

The eyes close. The Master's tongue explores his lips. He glares at the Under-Manager; uncaps his Swan fountain pen.

MASTER: Why didn't you tell me the man was sick, Papworth …?

Papworth's mouth moves wordlessly on the answer. Close shot Dunn's face, watching the pen; the pen, at work on the papers.

DUNN: *(calm)* Much obliged.

Long shot through glass doors of Poor Hospital ward, dark save for a single bed-lamp half-way down. A ward nurse comes out from the screened bed-area, carries a brown paper bag and a blanket towards the doors. Dunn and Gyp watch from the corridor.

NURSE: *(arriving; thick Manchester voice)* … There's his things. He'll sleep now.

DUNN: *(taking them)* Is he bad?

NURSE: Doctor says it's probly nobbut a chill, burr'e's frail and needs rest … *(She's been studying Gyp's bowler badge)* … Are you on this hunger march thing? *(Dunn nods)* Aye, I thought you were. Come back tomorrow morning, doctor'll know more then … *(She's on the move)*

DUNN: … Nurse. *(She turns)* No chance of bunking down on a bench somewhere, is there? Ah promised him he wouldn't be left.

NURSE: *(straight)* I didn't hear that, all right? *(She approaches a wall-lamp over a bench, turns down the flame to a dim glow)* Mind you, not seen's not known …

Gyp grins. The nurse leaves. Dunn takes the money-bag from his pocket, hands it to Gyp.

GYP: *(unconvincing)* <u>Ah</u>'ll stop if ye want, Jack …

DUNN: Nay, ah'll do it, Gyp.

GYP: *(relieved)* Ta. Gi' me the shivers. Ah'll come back early, 'case you've need o' me … *(He's leaving)*.

DUNN: Gyp. *(Gyp stops, sees the half of brandy in Dunn's hand. Returns for it)* Go easy.

They share a smile. Gyp nods, heads off. Dunn lays his gear and Percy's blanket on the darkened bench. Returns to the ward entrance. Stares in.

Slow panning gaze down the dark ward of sick old men, pummelled thin by progress, hacking and muttering a way through the night. Over this, trailed, Gyp's voice, quite pure, singing (A Pitman's Love Song):

Aw wish my love she was a grey ewe
Grazing by yonder river-side,
And aw mysel a bonny black tup;
Oh, on that ewie how aw would ride …

The scan ends on Percy's screens. A nurse arrives there. Turns out the light.

Night. Gyp leads Billy down the dark road back. He's stopped to take a swig on the bottle; keeps his eyes lifted, to take in the mist of stars above.

GYP: *(hushed)* World's changing, Bill. Head over heels.

Shot of cart, horse, man on move again, moon fat overhead. The song resumes:

Aw wish my lover was a ripe turd
Smokin' doon in yon dyke side
And aw mysel was a shitten flea;
Aw'd sook her all up before she was dried …

The cart clears frame; leaves the moon.

Cricket-hut. Michael Phelan, shirtless, stares bleakly out from the empty window-space, moonlit, spectral, unreal. Behind him, barely seen as she moves around the darkness, Ellen Pearson undresses for bed. Almost ready, she stands half-naked to watch him for a moment; dips eventually from frame to litter, the gap between them unfilled.

Slow inching barely perceptible track in on Phelan framed in the window. An owl hoots. A train, miles away, headed south, answers, wailing at the night.

PHELAN: *(voice over, low, bleak)* Dear loving woman, Forgive me for <u>writing</u> this goodbye: shame and desperation stop me saying it to your face. I have accepted that you may not ever have come to love me; but to reveal the black hole I'm in, and the things I've done to climb out, would fill your heart with such contempt, such revulsion, I could not bear it …

Thank you for these good weeks. What a great lot I have learned from you all … The glimpse of better days you gave me, you and all of you, Gyp, Will, Percy, Jack, I'll carry to my grave. Along with … *(Long silence. The track ends; his face, taut, ghastly, fills the shot; tears gleam from the dark of his eyes)* … the smell of your hair, the dance of your eyes, the warm give of your skin … the graveness, the purpose of you … Ellen. Ellen. Ellen. Ellen. I love you, I love the child within you, I love the future you carry in your stride, you and the journey one ... I leave the march to make amends. When ... if ... I'll come and find you. Till then, go well, go forward. A wee song for you ...

Silence. Tears grease cheeks, lips. He tastes them on his tongue.

ELLEN: *(over; low; distinct)* Michael. *(His face stills. Silence)* Look at me. Look at me.

He looks; can't but; a slow turn of the face, right, down; sees her.

PHELAN: *(overwhelmed)* O my ... lovely love ...

He stoops, to close with her. In the dark space, sounds of their loving, urgent and tender, spread slowly, filling the void. Cut to

Morning. Cricket ground. Close shot of Gyp's sleeping face. Billy's head bobs down into shot, lips and nostrils at work on the man's cheek. Gyp starts; wakes. The pony's head retracts.

GYP: Away, man. Let a body sleep.

Eyes close. Billy dips again. Trail sound of tapping, spoon on cup, and cut to

Morning. Hospital corridor. Close shot Jack Dunn, asleep on his bench. His eyes blink open, search out the sound. Focus finally on the nurse from last night standing over him.

DUNN: ... Is he ...?

NURSE: ... He's fine. Had a good night. Doctor's with him now. Here, drink your tea ...

He struggles upright, takes the cup and saucer, grateful. She places a towel and a bar of soap on the bench.

NURSE: There's a washroom at the bottom there ...

DUNN: Thank you.

She lays a handful of coins on the towel.

NURSE: ... We had a whip-round ... Night staff. Every little helps, as the old lady said as she widdled in the sea ...

Dunn's affected; seeks the words to tell her. She smiles; winks; leaves. He watches the swirl of cape and calf down the corridor for a moment, warmed by her. Cut to

Cricket-hut. Morning. Ellen Pearson, in close shot, back propped against

*the latted green pavilion, sits reading Phelan's letter again, face numbed,
for a moment lifeless.*

*A call from down the field. She looks. Gyp indicates the bucket he's
brought for her ablutions. She nods. Returns to the letter; the last page
again.*

PHELAN:
> *(voice over)* So we'll sing for tomorrow,
> If singing's no crime;
> And what's lacking we'll borrow
> From the slow jig of time.
> Sure, the roads may be parting,
> Given how the land lies;
> No more gentle sweethearting,
> No more dance to our eyes;
> Still we head for tomorrow,
> Still our reason to rhyme;
> Where we'll sing without sorrow
> To the sweet jig of time.

*She blinks, face pale, eyes grave, unhappy. In longer shot, the letter lies
limp in her fingers, head back and lifted, as if in pain. Cut to*

*Hospital. Corridor door to gardens, walkway. Jack Dunn watches Gyp
approach from trees. Behind him, at some distance by the gates, Ellen
waits with Billy and the cart.*

GYP: *(arriving)* … What's the word, comrade?

DUNN: Chill, they think. In a week or two he may be ready for some
marching … *(Scanning the gate area)* Michael?

GYP: Gone. Thin air. Left her a note. Upset her. *(Dunn frowns, uneasy.
Gyp hands him the moneybag, leadership resumed)* What's Percy say?

DUNN: Haven't been in yet. *(Silence)* Nurse says they'll keep him another
night, then discharge him to next door, vagrant's cell, like as not …

GYP: Nay, man …

DUNN: *(sharp)* Ah know. Ah know, Gyp. *(Sniffs. Thinks)* How's Billy?

GYP: Fine. *(Grins)* Strong as a horse.

Dunn nods. Pockets the money-bag. Picks up the brown paper bag.

DUNN: Ah'll have a word. Follow us round …

He points to the walkway on the outside of the ward, the glass door at its centre, disappears into the building. Gyp waves Ellen forward; released.

Ward. Percy Mann in close shot, propped, pale, weak, watches Dunn's purposeful approach down the ward.

PERCY: … Thought tha'd niver get 'ere, man …

DUNN: Overslept, Percy. Bad dreams. Nurse told me what's what. How do you feel?

PERCY: Feel fine. Feel fine.

DUNN: Good.

Percy rests, eyes half-closed. Dunn studies him with care, resolve thinning at Mann's palpable frailness; stares out of the window, sees Gyp advancing with the cart.

PERCY: *(low)* Leave me if ye have to, Jack. You're leading.

DUNN: *(slow)* That what you'd do, Perce?

PERCY: Me? Dinna ask <u>me</u>, man … Ah've allus been a crazy bugger …

Dunn nods at Gyp's wave through the window.

DUNN: The way I see it, Percy, if I have to leave you, it'll be with comrades, nothin' less … Meantime, if you fancy a ride, there's one waitin' for ye out there … *(he indicates the centre door. Lays the bag of clothes on the bedspread)* Now, if you think you can handle that … ye'd better start proving it.

Mann looks at the bag, Jack, the bag again. Dunn gives him nothing.

DUNN: … Ah'll have a word wi' the nurse.

He leaves for the corridor, quick, certain again. Percy sits upright, dizzies a little, eyes on the bag. Cut to

Hospital. Walkway, gardens. Shot of the centre door. Shot of the three, separate, separately centred, watching it. A clock strikes; quarter to. Dunn checks his watch. Shot of cart from the rear: Mann's litter waits. Billy flicks his head, restless; Gyp calls him quiet, one word. Ellen's face, watching the door. Jack's watching face. He turns, exchanges a look with Gyp. Gyp's face, watching.

Long remote shot of them, spread untidily around the institutional lawn and garden, for a moment caught in time.

Close shot of Ellen again: her eyes brighten.

GYP: *(over)* Old bugger.

Shot of the door, awkwardly opening. Percy Mann appears, dressed, blanket round shoulders. Clasps the rail guarding the steps. Stands for a moment, surveying the scene, finding his lungs after effort. Eventually:

PERCY: … Someone said someat about a ride goin' …

Gyp gathers Billy, brings the cart forward. Ellen helps Percy down the steps. Dunn watches. Movement slows, sound fades. Trail Dunn's journal voice over.

Slow mix to high vertical shot from above of a segment of tarmac road. The marchers enter frame singly: Jack Dunn; Ellen Pearson; Gyp leading Billy; the cart; Percy Mann under blankets on his litter.

DUNN: *(over)* Fortieth day out. The Irishman has gone, for good it would seem, and taken his troubles with him. He's missed, I think: a good man in the making … So we're down to four and a long haul ahead to find care and shelter for our sick comrade …

The frame's clear; road empty. Cut sound. An early forties army transport truck, framed but open, packed with trainee soldiers, noses into shot in their wake. Cut to

Sunset. Mute. They march, tiny, dark, profiled across a soft distant swag of Derbyshire hill. A blood-orange sun swells, sinks, beyond them.

DUNN: *(Journal; over)* … We head for Dunwell Main, the Pearson lass's home town, and hope of help. Percy hangs on … He knows – and we've accepted – he may yet die on us. But not without a shout; not him. If he does go, it'll be for the lack of not very much, God knows: food, rest, warmth, a proper place to be … Not very much, maybe; but the iron impossibilities of our lives, nonetheless …

They leave frame; sun's gone. In the silence, the slow remote pulsing drone of heavy warplanes invades the darkening scene.

Fade to black.

Caption: red on black: *'There is not a horse in England willing and able to work but has due food and lodging. And you say the same for our people is impossible? Brothers, I answer, if for you it be impossible, what is to become of you? It is impossible for us to believe it to be impossible. The human brain … refuses to believe in such impossibilities for Englishmen …'*

Thomas Carlyle: Past and Present 1843.

Mute. Fade up on shot of steps, plinth of small town war memorial, at this distance its text unreadable. Slow clarifying zoom in begins, moments before the marchers, legs, lower bodies, hooves and wheels, defocussed, at three-quarter speed, cross the frame. They clear; reveal the shot's arrived, the text readable: a list of the dead. Pan up, reading speed. Near the top: Dunwell Main; at the top, the granite image of a British Tommy and the dates commemorated: 1939-45. Fade to black.

Fade up on wide, low-angle shot of late forties working-class housing estate, from the centre of an active, sapling-lined, mid-afternoon street. Kids, bikes, mothers, the odd miner heading home from earlies; in the background, the pit-wheel, busy. The marchers register, small at the far end, advance as if unnoticed through the historic terrain. They grow, loom, wearing the year they've reached: demob suits, '39-'45 campaign medals; at once <u>in</u> time and from it. Gypsy's last, earring, pigtail, bowler intact within the shift: continuities far deeper than fashion.

They've stopped; stare up at something in silence. On the reverse, we see Dunwell Main colliery notice-board, perched by the Main Gate. The legend contains part of the proclamation of nationalisation, the aims and purposes of the National Coal Board. Shots of their faces as they read.

Slow mix to

Afternoon; sunlit. Slow pan of late '40s NHS hospital frontage from above, across unfinished wings to active Main Entrance and on along a pathway linking perimeter road and building, against a tide of visitors headed for the wards. Halfway along, unremarked in the moil, Dunn and Gyp carry Mann towards Reception. The shot ignores them, scans on unhurriedly for the gate, reaches Ellen Pearson, Billy's bridle in her hand, reading the large proud new hospital board; holds for some moments on her reading face. Cut to

The board she reads: another historic inscription.

Over much of this, remote, wild-tracked, Dunn and Gyp reassure and cajole the resistant Mann.

Slow mix to

Secondary Modern School, a year old. Long track along corridors, stairways, as Ellen Pearson and Dunn follow an old one-armed caretaker into the active heart of the place. Sounds, images, lively, purposive, invade their passage.

CARETAKER: *(a sour, stolid, intermittent mutter throughout)* ... You'da stood all day if you'da stood by her office, she's never there ... They can do art they want at this place ... Nart like this in my day, I'll tell you ...

Jack shares a smile with Ellen, who's a touch tense now, as they approach the Art Room ahead.

CARETAKER: You'll find 'er in there, like as not ... She'll be art in a minute'r two ... *(He glares through the window)* Lookar'em standin' on them bloody benches, the bloody 'eadmistress in the room ... See what ah mean? Pardon the language.

He makes to shuffle off.

ELLEN: ... It sounds as if you don't find her ... all that good ...

CARETAKER: *(turning; distinct)* Eh. You're not them Daily Mail people back again are you? *(Riding through her attempt at answer)* She's not ... good, missy: she's <u>great</u>. And ah'll 'ear no argument on the matter. Tell that to your bloody readers, as if you would, communist or not, you'll scour the country and not find a ...

ELLEN: *(gently)* ... We're not press ...

He sniffs.

CARETAKER: ... I just don't like 'avin' a woman for a boss, s'all that's wrong wi' me ...

He hobbles away. A bell rings. The door ahead opens, a woman in her early fifties, iron-haired, firm-voiced, the knob in her hand, holds the massing ranks of fourteen year olds at bay in the doorway, waiting a moment for order. A Craven A hangs from her mouth.

WOMAN: *(factual; no tonal shift)* ... Group project reports due in Friday, leaders please note ... Mural people, good work, pottery people good but slow, work harder ... We need to talk about the banner work, there's something not right ... Martin Crowe, do that once more and your backside and my stick will be having an argument ... Right, take your break ...

She makes way; they leave. She exchanges thoughts, observations en passant, respectful, at ease.

Ellen watches her intently, keen to be seen, yet fearing to presume the welcome she needs. Kids drain past them. The woman follows them with her eyes; sees the two figures; drops her prescription glasses from forehead to eyes to make them out.

ELLEN: *(low-voiced)* Hello, mum …

A moment. They stare at each other.

MOTHER: Hello, my love …

She holds her arms out; Ellen advances for the hug. Dunn's face, watching. Rills of their sotto exchanges – 'You got my letter?' … 'Everything's arranged' … reach him remotely. Eventually, Ellen's mother takes him smilingly in over her daughter's shoulder, both still deep inside the tough, needful embrace. He smiles back, grave, shy.

MAN'S VOICE: *(trailed from next scene; over)* … It's no use talkin' with 'em, brothers, these people are communists, agents of a foreign creed, and many of 'em of a foreign power into the bargain …

Listeners mutter; cut to

Mid-evening. Trades Council Club. A grizzled man in his mid-sixties, short, overweight, on his feet, addresses the several dozen delegates arrayed untidily before him in a meeting room designed for fewer. A stocky, bald-headed man chairs the meeting; a third man, in demob suit, shares the table.

MAN (ARTHUR POINTER): *(over critical comment)* … Oh yes, and we've proved it … As I say, it's no use talkin' with 'em, they don't believe in democracy so they wouldn't understand what you're talkin' about … That's why I supported our Labour Government last year when it invoked the Emergency Powers Act and sent in troops to break the illegal strike in the London docks … And that's why I'm supporting them this year too, ditto …

He stops, belly resting on the trestle table he talks from, pours water on the scotch he's just been served, downs it. In the doorway, Jack Dunn watches, a crowded and lively bar-area in the room behind him.

DELEGATE: *(dry; from back)* S'nart but blue suits and shirts sin' ye got darn there, Arthur …

ARTHUR: … Ah'll pint thee under t'table any day'er the week, brother … Thi's likely not reached thi prostrate yet, but thi will … *(Laughter. The critic joins it.)* … Let nobody be in any doubt, this is the same Arthur Pointer you sent down four year ago, a workin' man, proud of 'is class and eager to see it prosper …

LISTENER: … Aye, an' 'ow about the bloody wage-freeze you've stuck on us, then …?

ARTHUR: … Ah'm comin' to that, brother, ah'm comin' to that …

CHAIRMAN: *(seated by him; a tough sphinx)* … You've got six minutes, Arthur …

ARTHUR: … Yes I know, Peter, but I'll not 'ave people sayin' I've …

CHAIRMAN: *(implacable)* … You promised to say something about the next election …

ARTHUR: … Aye, and I will. I will.

He picks up his tumbler, finds it empty; looks for help; finds none; pours a water. Jack Dunn watches. The chairman's eyes move towards him; hold. Dunn returns the gaze. A long steady contact.

ARTHUR: *(gathering)* … Brothers, four years ago, when we came to power, we never said it's goin' to be heaven tomorrow, we knew better than anyone the democratic road to socialism would be a long and a hard one … But in less than one parliament, we've turned this country upside down … *(applause; agreement)* Nothin'll ever be the same again … National coal, national railways, national insurance, national health, national gas and electricity, national steel on the way … Full employment. Think of it. For the first time in our history … . Do you know how many people died of hunger in this land last year? None. Do you know how many expired from an illness they couldn't afford to have treated? None. That's the country we've been buildin', brothers … And we're ready to go on till the job's finished … *(more applause)* Now, the Major up there *(his thumb indicates the painting of Attlee in miner's helmet on the wall behind)* has so far failed to consult me on the date of the next election, as it happens … *(laughter)* bur' ah'll tell ye this, lads, it'll be sooner rather than later, and when it comes, ah'll be at his bloody shoulder … as ah hope you'll be at mine …

Another scotch has arrived. He goes through his watering ritual, readjusts the swag of his belly back inside his blue serge waistband. Jack Dunn sips on his pint, withdraws into the bar-room; the MP's voice dogs him a second or two longer as he crosses the room.

ARTHUR: *(over; fading)* … In '45 we found a new slogan: We are the Masters now … And we've got to win again, so that we can proudly say – and know it's true, by God – We are the Masters still …

Bar area. The spray of applause follows Dunn towards Gypsy Armstrong, spruced for a night, deep in talk with a young, bright-eyed barwoman.

Dunn watches his comrade at work; loves him. The woman's called to serve; Gyp drinks deep from his pint; sees Jack down the bar. Grins.

DUNN: All right?

GYP: Oh aye. What d'your man want?

DUNN: Haven't talked. S'got a meeting …

The barwoman passes by, gives Gyp a wink. Gyp twiddles his earring; happy.

DUNN: Find your way back, will ye …?

GYP: Aye. If ah have to …

Jack's eyes wander around the busy room. Miners sit in gaggles, drinking, talking, on their way home. The meeting's breaking up; delegates head for the bar. He moves on; sees, through an open door, a billiard table, not in use, under a strong light.

MAN: Jack Dunn, is it?

Dunn turns; finds the bald-headed chairman, hand powerfully out for his. Dunn gives it.

TAMS: Peter Tams, Area Secretary, NUM.

DUNN: Good to meet you. *(indicating)* Andy Armstrong …

TAMS: *(a nod)* How are ye? … *(to Dunn)* Lily Stone mentioned you might be passin' through … Got a coupla minutes …?

DUNN: Surely …

TAMS: *(to barwoman; indicating meeting room)* … Two bitters, Rita, when you've a sec …

He leads Dunn off, quick, organised, authoritative. Amstrong watches Rita pull the pints.

GYP: Gi' ye some muscles, this job, won't it?

She looks at him quite frankly for a moment, still teasing the ale from the pump.

RITA: Does it give ye bother …?

GYP: Nay.

RITA: *(traying the pints)* Good. 'Cos I come as I come …

She leaves the bar with the tray. He watches her over the rim of his glass.

Meeting room. A man's stacking chairs against a wall. A last clutch of delegates beards the MP by the table. The man in the demob suit shoves papers and pamphlets into his battered leather case. Sees Tams and Dunn approaching.

MAN: *(Welsh voice)* Why don't you buy the lads a drink, Arthur? I'll join you in a minute …

ARTHUR: Aye, come on, lads, no rest for the wicked, eh …?

He leads them out. Tams nods the chair-clearer to finish, click out the surplus lights, leave. The three are left lit, in the shadowed room.

TAMS: Jack Dunn, Ellis Evans. *(Nods exchanged)* Take a seat … *(He swings round as the door re-opens: Rita carries the tray to the table) … Thanks. Put the sign up, will ye, love …

RITA: *(nods; lays pints out; trays empties)* Elsie's not in and I'm due off in …

TAMS: *(not interested)* Have a word with Geoff, will ye, sweetheart …?

RITA: *(a beat)* Aye … All right, darlin' …

She leaves. Tams frowns briefly, dealing with the women problem; Dunn glances up at the helmeted Major.

TAMS: *(eventually)* Ellis is Labour Party Regional Organizer. Ellis?

EVANS: Aye. *(He looks at Dunn briefly, then down at the form he's taken from the bag)* Heard you speak at the Durham Gala last year. Liked what I heard. And Peter says the Union word on you is you're a bit likely … *(He pushes the form across the table: Dunn reads it briefly, looks at Tams, who sits impassive; at Evans, who watches him evenly)* Peter'll fill you in on details, I've got another …

The door opens again, the grizzled MP slops round the noticed door, glass in hand.

ARTHUR: … Ellis, d'you think the Knockley thing's necessary? I'm just as 'appy stoppin' 'ere …

He stops, sways a touch, focuses on the three-man meeting; frowns, uneasy.

EVANS: *(unhurried)* Knockley's important, Arthur. Finish that and we'll go …

Arthur nods. Thinks.

ARTHUR: I think ah need another pee.

He leaves. Silence. Evans' face is flint as he watches the door close.

EVANS: ... Look, if I don't get the bugger over to Knockley, I'll be drivin' him there in a bucket ... Peter'll explain the position, whatever he tells you goes wi' me too ... All I'll need to know is you've no ... ideological objection to joinin' ... *(He indicates the form on the table: in closer shot, we see it's an application for membership of the Labour Party)* Good to meet you ...

DUNN: Aye.

EVANS: *(on his way)* ... See you Thursday, Peter, GMC.

TAMS: Thursday. Aye.

He's gone. Dunn takes a pull on his beer. Lifts the form from the table a touch, inquiringly. Tams moves to the chair on the other side of the table, sits, to face him.

TAMS: An' 'ave ye? *(He waits)* Any ideological objection to ...?

DUNN: *(calm)* ... Yes, I know what ye're askin' ... Ah'm not sure I have an answer ... in a void ...

Silence. They look at each other.

TAMS: All right. There's people around think you're wasting your time and your talent wi' that lot ... *(He points to Dunn's campaign march badge)* ... I'm one of 'em. Industrial democracy? Workers' self-management? Reorganization of the mining industry? Fine. One day. No problems. But now? Wi' the load we've got on our plates?

DUNN: *(slow; measured)* Ah'm fightin' the front ah'm facin', comrade.

TAMS: *(deliberate)* That's as mebbe, comrade. But you're needed elsewhere.

Silence.

DUNN: *(quiet)* Where's that?

TAMS: Here, to start with. There's a job goin' at Regional NUM, workin' wi' me on the election, start right away. And before you tell me you're black-listed and can't get a pit job to qualify, I know ... and it can be got round.

Dunn absorbs what he can. None of it has been expectable.

DUNN: *(the form)* And this?

TAMS: One of our seats'll be up soon. Ashbourne. With management, in time for next year's election.

Long pause. Dunn deals with it.

DUNN: Ah thought Arthur Pointer …

TAMS: … With luck, he'll be announcing his unwillingness to stand at the next election. Without, we'll deselect him. He's back now testing his strength … He hasn't yet quite grasped, it's nothing personal … Listen, comrade, the next five years are going to be decisive for the whole working class of this country … and the principal site of struggle for the direction of those five years is gonna be parliament. And given the … slippage that's been goin' on down there lately … and the cast-iron certainty of a vastly reduced majority … a certain feeling's grown up that maybe replacing the damp union-fodder that Arthur – and scores like him, union-sponsored – have become with people who'll do the job that's needed wouldn't be all that bad an idea …

He stops, as if winded by the rills of his argument. Dunn grins, enjoying it now, some shy, wary respect flowing between them.

TAMS: Fact is, people who'll do the job needed down there aren't that numerous … Parliamentary cretinism's an endemic contagion that strikes down all but the best. *(Pause)* I'm prepared to stake you have immunity …

Long silence. A woman of about 40 pops her head round the door.

WOMAN: … Rita's off, says she needs her money …

TAMS: Thanks, Elsie.

She leaves. Silence again. Tams stands, folds the application form, pocket-size, hands it to Dunn.

TAMS: You've too much upstairs not to be thinkin' about it … Lily'll tell you where I can be got. *(Hand out)* Go easy, eh?

Dunn stands. Takes the hand.

DUNN: Thanks.

Tams leaves. Dunn stares at the Major for a moment; follows him out.

Bar. Dunn stands, checking for Gypsy. Evans helps Arthur into his coat and hat. Arthur's glass changes hands as his arms go in. Tams talks with Rita by the street door about her working conditions. A fair-haired miner pours ale into a saucer for his whippet, whispering to it in Polish. Gypsy's gone.

Ellen's mother's house – the family pit-cottage. Bedroom. Night. Mirror shot of a woman's profiled belly, a soft five-month show. Slow pan up to the face of Ellen, studying it.

Sound of van, door slamming, voices in the street below. Ellen glances out of the window briefly, resuming her skirt. Stands in her girlhood bedroom in silence for some moments; refeels the past.

Images of her scan of walls, surfaces: photographs, people, her life; dolls from childhood; a framed teaching certificate; a strange wrought-iron crucifix, Christ the Miner hanging from it.

HER FATHER'S VOICE: *(in the room)* God's dead, luvvie. Like minin'.

A key scricks in the front door. Ellen walks to the stairhead. In close shot, unseen, she watches her mother rest a moment, half-shadowed, eyes closed, before passing into the lit kitchen.

MOTHER: *(calling)* I'm back, love. How was the hospital?

ELLEN: *(on the move, calling)* They're doing tests. They'll keep him a fortnight, they say … build him up. *(She's back in her bedroom, before the mirror)* How was your meeting?

MOTHER: *(calling)* Fine. You want Horlicks?

ELLEN: Mmm.

Silence. Ellen studies her skirted belly in the glass.

MOTHER: You want to talk?

A moment.

ELLEN: *(Face, close shot)* Surely.

Silence again.

PHELAN'S VOICE: *(in the room)* … Why should it matter … if I want you … and you want me?

Slow mix, over Ellen's reflected image, to

Night. A huge expanse of old, limed slagheaps, irregularly lit by slung lamps: moon-terrain. Slow inching track in on Billy and the cart, at the still heart of the place. Sounds of love-making, passion voiced, gradually invade the silence.

The shot arrives at the cart: Gyp and Rita lie naked under a blanket in the back, need and desire urgent in both of them; moves on, beyond them, to Billy, head down in the shafts, tugging at clumps of burdock improbably seeded along a trackway.

A train screeches, approaching a distant tunnel. Billy stirs, startled; pulls the cart slowly into motion. Behind him, love sounds go on unchecked; oblivious.

In long shot, pony and cart wander the silent moonscape. Mixing to

Night. A watery image of Arthur Pointer, ex-miner MP. A small spray of gravel disperses the reflection. Pan up canal bridge to a hand, still half-filled with stones; and on, to Jack Dunn, brooding down at the dark water from the lamplit bridge.

Water again, settling: fragments of a new reflection begin to form. Dunn's face, watching, intent. He stands up abruptly, showers the rest of the gravel on the water, walks off, as if angry. The shot pans to follow his progress into the dark of the town; returns slowly to the bridge, the water as it stills again. The image that's unsettled him will not go away: Dunn, head cropped, eyes fierce, as he was in '27.

Wind frets at the image.

ELLEN'S MOTHER: *(over; trailed)* ... These are good. Mmm.

Kitchen. Close shot of a sketch-pad being studied: images of the march. Ellen's mother's face, assessing the work.

Down the table, Ellen nurses her Horlicks, toys inattentively with a sheaf of printed papers. Her mother notes the disinterest.

MOTHER: ... See anything you like?

ELLEN: ... I'm not experienced enough for most of them ...

MOTHER: ... You're a graduate, girl, we're crying out for people like you ...

Ellen sips her Horlicks doggedly. Her mother turns a page: a pencil sketch of Jack Dunn, reading by lamplight.

MOTHER: Nell, I know how bad the last months must have been for you ... Frank falling sick ... the shock of his death ... finding you were carrying his child ... And I understand absolutely what pushed you to take his place on the march ... But you can't ... wander the country for ever, there's work to be done. Six months, a year, the whole lot's up for auction again. We have to dig in, at every level, the gains our people have made have got to be defended, not a single one of them is irreversible. *(She looks down again at the reading Dunn)* It's just not the time to be marching on London demanding the impossible. Personally or politically. *(She waits. Ellen sits on)* I want to help, Nell. At least talk about it …

Ellen leaves the table, crosses to the fireplace, stares at a framed photograph of her father kissing a pigeon on the beak. Her mother watches her a moment, returns to marking her heap of exercise books by her elbow.

ELLEN: *(quiet; sudden)* Do you still miss him?

MOTHER: *(eventually; working on)* Now and again.

Close shot of the miner's face, warm, open.

ELLEN: *(over; quoting, his voice)* 'Penny for yer thoughts … '

Lily looks up at her. Eventually:

MOTHER: *(his voice too)* '… Twopence for yer feelin's.'

She turns, shares a smile.

ELLEN: I wouldn't know where to start …

MOTHER: One place is as good as another …

ELLEN: *(almost sharp)* It's not <u>it</u>, Lily, it's <u>you</u> … Everything's so … organised in you, life, politics, feelings, practice, all bound up together, classified … known about … To tell you something is to be … judged by all that; measuring up or being found wanting … It's not a way I want to talk any longer …

Silence, edged, uncertain; little eye-contact. Ellen collects her discarded sketch-pad from her mother's end of the table, returns to her seat at the other. Flicks the pages, randomly; Will, Percy Mann, Gyp and Billy; stops at the last entry: Michael Phelan, naked, on a river bank, in gladed sunlight.

Over this, out of shot, low-voiced:

MOTHER: *(simply)* I've changed a bit myself, love. Talk how you will.

The two women look at each other for some time. Ellen returns to the sketch-book: the first image, a charcoal drawing of a one-armed miner asleep in a chair by the fire, inscribed FRANK PEARSON (1917-1949).

ELLEN: Lily … Everything's so … strange just now … In movement.

Beyond theory, somehow. *(Long pause)* Frank's death released so many things in me ... These last months have been ... bad, you called them ... no ... extraordinary. Transforming. Frightening ... Everything's important suddenly, every part of my life challenged, every part of myself reclaimable, reworkable. *(Pauses; sorting it out)* This ... action, this march ... defines me anew, every mile we cover ... Gives me comrades ... Takes me to the edge of something ... a new politics, a new practice, a new ... person ... *(She finds the drawing of Phelan again, looks at it. He stands arms folded, unafraid in his nakedness, smiling at her)* I have no plans, Lily. After London ... perhaps I'll go back to school and learn how to paint, I might do that ...

MOTHER: *(soft)* With a child? On your own? How will you live ...?

ELLEN: ... I'll find out, can't wait to, that's the point of it all. I know in your ears it sounds like drift, it <u>isn't</u>, it's not how it feels, it feels like real movement, away from, towards ... *(Long silence)* If you want to help, mum: just bless the journey.

They look at each other, eyes deep, serious. In the silence, next door's wireless asserts itself: an Irish tenor singing Danny Boy.

A tap at the back window: Jack Dunn's face peers in above the curtain, withdraws discreetly into darkness. Ellen stands to let him in. Lily catches her hand as she passes, holds it for a moment without speaking or looking, finally releases it. The shot rests with her. Sounds of Jack in scullery. She stands, heads for the bedding trunk in the hall, takes out blankets, a towel, returns as Jack and Ellen enter the kitchen.

MOTHER: ... Come in, comrade, I never finished making up the front room ...

DUNN: *(reaching for the gear)* ... Nay, ah'll do all that ...

MOTHER: ... Sit you down, there's tea in the pot, I'll be but a minute ...

She leaves for the front room. Ellen hands down a mug from a shelf, pours him tea. He stands, uneasy, uncertain, a touch preoccupied.

ELLEN: Sit down.

DUNN: Nay, you were talkin' ...

ELLEN: It's all right.

He sits at table. Fiddles with his pipe. She places the tea by him, returns to her chair to face him.

DUNN: Did you see Perce?

ELLEN: He's fine. In his element. He's organised a ward committee, got himself elected shop steward ... *(His question hangs)* A fortnight, they say. *(Dunn nods)* He's ... in good hands, Jack.

He sips his tea. Broods a little.

ELLEN: Gyp coming ...?

DUNN: Aye. Later. *(Pause)* He met a lass.

She looks at him. He looks away.

ELLEN: Did you get through to the Cardiff people?

DUNN: Aye. *(She waits. He's seen the sketch of Phelan; stares at it)* ... They'll contact us nearer the time ... just to be safe ... They're worried about police informers and telephone taps like everybody else ...

ELLEN: *(the drawing)* It's Michael. Do you like it?

DUNN: *(slowly)* It's good. Aye. The er ... National Union's finally agreed to defend the Scots lads. They're still in gaol ...

He looks as if there's more to be said. Says nothing. Lily returns from the front room. Jack gets up, mug in hand.

MOTHER: You don't have to go ...

DUNN: ... Ah have things to do ...

MOTHER: Oh, I carried father's tool-box through, I hope it has what you need ...

DUNN: Thanks.

He leaves for the front room. Lily stands inside the door a moment. Ellen slowly closes the book on Phelan.

ELLEN: Mum ...

MOTHER: ... Bless you, Nell.

A moment.

ELLEN: *(released)* Oh mum ...

Lily moves to the table, takes her daughter's face to her belly, hugs her fiercely in her big hands. Ellen laughs, crying.

MOTHER: ... You know something, love? Every brain in my head tells me it's wrong, you're wrong ... and all I can <u>feel</u> is: I wish I were going with you ...

ELLEN: *(laughing, crying)* Come. What's stopping you …?

Lily draws her upright, holds her face in her hands. Kisses her gently.

MOTHER: I have work. There are children depending on me … Go to bed.

Ellen kisses her on the cheek, moves to collect her sketch-pad.

MOTHER: Leave me that, will you.

Ellen smiles. Lays it down, closed, on the table.

MOTHER: Thanks.

Ellen nods. Leaves. Lily looks at the pad. Reaches for it. Opens it. Flicks on towards the back. Arrives at the final sketch. The naked man, strongly and clearly drawn, stares out at her.

Bring up guitar introduction to song and mix to

Night. Slow hovering image of a stretch of common overlooking Dunwell Main, at the colliery end of town. Lines of gaunt pit cottages glint below. Billy and cart come into view, secured where the wander ended by a low limestone wall.

Over, Phelan sings, guitar and flute for company:

PHELAN'S SONG:
> So we'll sing for tomorrow
> If singing's no crime;
> And what's lacking we'll borrow
> From the slow jig of time
>
> Etc.

The shot has found the far side of the cart, where Gyp and Rita sit propped against a wheel, clothed again. Song, shot, end on Rita's face.

RITA: *(half as if to camera)* … God'll have to forgive me for sayin' it, but I look back at that time, millions dead and maimed, suffering and destruction, lives ruined … and I know *(she works it out)* … I'll never have as good a time again. *(Shivers a little at the cold thought)* I'd done six years in service, straight from school, on'y job goin', three pound fifteen a week and 'alf a cold attic for home … And overnight I'm learnin' a real job, I'm learnin' a trade, I'm toolin' shell cases in a munitions factory, I've ten pound a week clear and a little flat o' me own in Derby … *(She stops: feels the power of that past)* For the first time in my life I was … in chargea meself … I was at the centrea things. *(Long silence)* The war gave me that. And the peace took it back. Into the cage with yer, woman. Wed, cook, bear, serve. *(Pause)* No thanks. Not me. I tasted someat. I'll have more of it.

Long shot of the two, framed by the cart. Rita strokes the hair around his ears.

RITA: *(Perspectived sound; almost wild track)* Why do they call you Gypsy? Is it this?

GYP: Ah reckon so, aye.

RITA: Why do you wear it?

GYP: My dad wore it. So did his.

He draws deep on a bottle of brown ale. She shoves a hand in his chest.

RITA: You think I'm crackers, don't you …

GYP: *(resisting)* … Ah don't …

RITA: *(reaching for the bottle)* … Y'aven't the foggiest what I'm talkin' about, 'ave yer …

He holds her off, finishes his swig. Hands it to her. Wipes his lips. She laughs.

RITA: … I coulda died when you said you 'ad transport …

He laughs with her. They look at each other; kiss, quite hard.

GYP: Ah know well enough what ye're talkin' about, love. Ye've seen the hover of the hawk. Ye'll not crawl again.

Silence.

RITA: Where is it you come from again?

GYP: County Durham?

RITA: Many hawks up there, are there?

GYP: One or two.

They kiss again. The shot holds. Trail sounds of irregular hammering. Mix to

Pit-cottage. Front room, lit by single table lamp. Slow arhythmic pan of the walls and surfaces. Images of family, practice: a late '20s painted tea-set; pics of Ellen's parents; the seven-year-old girl on her dad's knee. The scan takes in a mantel-mirror. In it, we glimpse Jack Dunn in the room, hammering at something between his feet. Two framed teaching certificates loom: Lily's, Ellen's. A pic of Ellen and Frank's wedding. A flock mattress made up on the floor; a sofa, ditto.

Pan gradually to Dunn, at work hammering a shaped patch of curved leather onto the sole of a boot: lip, hand, hammer. The work is angry but accurate; intense; will-filled.

He lays the hammer down, reaches into the wooden tool-box for a rasp. Begins working on the boot's edges.

Lily's head appears round the hall door. Dunn gets to his feet, rasp and boot in hands.

DUNN: Is it the noise? Ah'll be done in a tick …

MOTHER: No, no, I'm going up, I've left the door on the latch for your friend …

DUNN: Thanks. Comrade.

She dwells a moment in the doorway.

MOTHER: How was your meeting? Did they offer?

DUNN: Aye.

MOTHER: Arthur Pointer there? *(He nods)* You can see what they mean …

DUNN: Aye, there's a few around … Good lives rottin' before they've ripened …

MOTHER: Arthur went down with ammunition and turned into fodder. It has to be put right. A lot of serious socialists think it's a high priority. *(She waits. He says nothing. She smiles)* Did you say no at once, or will you let them know?

He looks at her, sees the smile, looks down at the boot on his fist, the repairing rasp in the other hand.

DUNN: *(A smile)* Ah suppose ah'll let them know. *(Pause)* Ah could tell you why, I don't know how much sense it'd mek to you … *(Another pause)* Ah knew a man who'd met Lenin, Third International Congress. Talked to him over a pint. Asked him for a slogan, to bring back to his comrades in Durham. Lenin said – ah don't know the French for it, that's what they were talkin': Think the impossible. Demand the impossible. Be a realist.

MOTHER: *(Eventually)* Lenin?

DUNN: Accordin' ter Jackie Hartley.

Silence. She nods. Shares his smile.

MOTHER: Look after that one, will you? *(Her finger points upwards. He nods)* She's important.

DUNN: Ah know.

MOTHER: Go well.

DUNN: You too.

She leaves, closes the door behind her. He listens to her step on the stair. Turns, sees himself reflected in the dark mirror. Over:

DUNN:'S VOICE: *(Reading; internal)* … But I warn you labourers, work while you have the chance, for Hunger is coming fast and shall awake with the floods to deal justice on wastrels …

The reflection has faded, revealing a later one: Jack Dunn in his sofa bed, reading by lamplight. Slow zoom into reflection. Over:

DUNN'S VOICE: *(Reading; internal)* … The poorest folk are our neighbours, if we look about us – the prisoners in dungeons and the poor in their hovels, overburdened with children, and rack-rented by landlords … I've seen enough of the world to know how they suffer, these men … and no means but their trade to clothe and feed them. For many hands are waiting to grasp the few pence they earn …

The shot has closed on the reflected image. He lays the book down, switches off the lamp, settles down to sleep. The shot ends on the faintly lit copy of Piers the Ploughman.

Front room. The book, as before. Dunn breathes deep, regular; asleep. His face, pale in the dark. A noise in the room, something falling; a curse. The eyes open fast, struggle with vision.

GYP: S'on'y me. Dropped me boot …

Dunn peers, can't see him, slips a hand out, clicks on the lamp. Gypsy stands in shadow in underpants, vest, socks. Finds his litter. Climbs into it.

GYP: Ta.

Dunn clicks off the lamp. The thinnest smear of streetlamp lightens the heavy dark of the room: from here, the scene's mainly sound.

Silence.

DUNN: The lass saw Percy.

GYP: *(Slow)* Aye?

DUNN: They'll keep him a while. *(No answer)* How was your evenin'?

GYP: *(Slow)* ... Ah had a good time.

Silence. Dunn stares through the gloom; can't see his comrade's face. Senses something.

DUNN: You all right, Gyp?

Long silence.

GYP: Aye, ah'm fine.

They shuffle on to their sides to sleep. Silence. Close shot Dunn's face, eyes lidded.

GYP: Maybe ah'll wait till old Perce's better, bring 'im on ...

The lids open. The grave eyes grapple with his meaning. Slow fade to black.

A burst of organ music (Caption: Coronation Day, 1953) swells, falls to silence. Fade up long lens shot along an empty stretch of road. Ahead, the road disappears abruptly, the brow of a hill; soft midland miles of distant country fill the rest of the shot.

Sounds of marching, stud on tarmac, grow in the hazy summer silence. Bereted heads, rows of three, inch above the road; young men's faces; battledress; full kit: a platoon of national service conscripts on basic-training route march. Three NCOs bark their exhortatory litany from the sidelines, wildtrack, at the sweat of kids heading nowhere.

LITANY: *(Shared)* ... Stretch out at the front there, this is s'posed to be a route march, not a fuckin' meander ... Take that man's name, corporal ... No, the long streak o' piss in the middle there ... Look at his fucking rifle, man, just look at it ... Left *(beat)* left *(beat)* left right left ... Open your legs at the front, I said ... You think you're gonna lose someat? Forget it, you've nothin' up there worth 'angin' on to anyway ... Every time I look at you festering spunkbags I hear a sound and you know what that sound is it's the sound of half a million slimy communist wogs in the jungles of Malaya RUBBIN' THEIR HANDS TOGETHER ... WITH <u>RELISH</u> ... the first time they clap eyes on you lot ... In step, in step, you're out of STEP, twathead ... Save the Empire? You lot couldn't save your fuckin' breath ... MOVE ...

The platoon and its harriers crush through the shot. The litany fades to nothing. The shot holds on the cleared road.

DUNN'S JOURNAL: *(voice over)* Forty-ninth day out and headed for
   Oxford. Comrade Mann stays in Dunwell, with march money to bring
   him down later, if he's fit.

*He crests the hill by inches. Marches deep into the shot. Behind, some
way, cresting separately, Ellen appears.*

DUNN'S JOURNAL: *(voice over)* ... The lass goes from strength to strength.
   She's proving a real comrade ...

He's gone. Ellen follows. The road's empty again.

DUNN'S JOURNAL: *(voice over)* ... But I think we're both missing Gyp and
   Billy ...

Fast burst of coronation music and cut to

*Black and white television image. Fisher raises the coronation crown,
heavy with rubies. Cries of Vivat from the Lords' pews. The head is
crowned. Shots pick out the era's luminaries: Churchill's prominent in
Gilbert and Sullivan costume of the Warden of the Cinque Ports.
Dimbleby lovingly dubs him 'our beloved prime minister' ...*

*Slow pan of watching faces in a crowded country town bar; Jack Dunn's
among them, on the fringes, a tray of beers and sandwiches in his hand.
Murmurs of 'God bless her' 'Radiant' 'Makes you feel proud' ripple across
the moil of suited solicitors, estate agents, auctioneers and gentlemen
farmers crowding the best room. Dunn threads a silent way to the door.*

*Cobbled front of inn. People sit at trestled tables, inventing an
impromptu coronation party. Union Jacks hang from the inn windows.
Over the door, a large red, white and blue banner proclaims 'God Save
the Queen' directly over the inn-sign: 'The Old Cow'. Dunn emerges,
carries his tray through the tables to the corner of the building.*

*Ellen Pearson sits on a grass verge, shoes and socks off, working in her
sketch-pad. Dunn arrives, lays the tray down, joins her on the grass.
Bawled loyal toasts, snatches of 'There'll always be an England' and
'Rule Britannia' carry from the inn-front.*

*Ellen takes her pint and sandwich, continues with her work. Dunn eats,
sups, a touch inturned.*

ELLEN: Get through?

DUNN: *(Blinking)* Aye. He says they're frettin' about a shadda or someat
   on the lung ...

She stops working to look at him.

DUNN: ... He's chirpy enough. Fifty years o' coaldust, norra shadda at all, he says, pointless to operate, they'd be better off nationalisin' it ...

She chuckles. He smiles.

ELLEN: *(Grave)* Shit.

DUNN: Aye.

Dunn eats on. Ellen returns to her pad.

ELLEN: Gyp?

DUNN: Visits every day. Takes his lass wi' 'im ...

ELLEN: That why he stayed, you think? *(Dunn says nothing. She works on)* You miss him, don't you.

Dunn sniffs; washes the sandwich down with beer.

DUNN: Aye. But we mek our own beds.

A conga of loyal revellers edges beyond the inn building, wanders along the roadway in front of them. They watch for a moment. People wave them to join. A man in blazer, cravat, slacks, looms soddenly before them from the maul, gin in hand.

MAN: Rejoice. Civic duty, man ...

DUNN: *(Brief)* Ahunh. We're havin' our lunch.

MAN: ... We're patriots, you see. Loyal subjects ...

DUNN: So ah see.

MAN: *(Fuddling)* Not good enough ... Whole country's on its feet with joy and you sit here ...

DUNN:

> *(fierce; fast)* ... 'Last came Anarchy: he rode
> On a white horse splashed with blood;
> He was pale even to the lips,
> Like Death in the Apocalypse.
> And he wore a kingly crown;
> And in his grasp a sceptre shone;
> On his brow this mark I saw –
> I AM GOD, AND KING, AND LAW.'

> Go away.

The revelling gent rocks gently in front of them for some moments, fumily sensing the dog turd he's stepped in.

MAN: *(finally)* God save the Queen, by God.

He reels away, clasps at a conga-ing woman's hips as she passes.

ELLEN: *(Dry)* Shelley? *(He sniffs)* I didn't think you read poetry.

DUNN: I read all sorts. Bin' readin' Shelley since ah were a kid.

He's gathering stuff for the tray. Hunkers forward to see her page. She works on in silence.

DUNN: Don't mind me lookin', d'ye …? *(She shakes her head, absorbed. Suddenly:)* Easter Sunday. Bloody 'ell. There's old Will …

She pulls back to give him a better view. Close in on the drawing: it's the Cowman's Dinner, powerfully recovered in pencil, alive with the grave pleasure of the meal.

DUNN: *(savouring it)* My God … S'how it was …

They march south, through a fat, green Warwickshire and a montage of images, captions, quotes, archive materials and witnesses' voiced experience essentialising the fifties. Shards of a political, social, cultural history emerge: the recrudescence of British and world capital, the re-emergence of ruling class parties, the construction of admass consumerism and cold war stratifications, the willed creation of the Third World, the emplacement of nuclear industries; together with the gathering forms of critical moral response and popular resistance. Rock and roll, television, teddy boys begin to occupy the equivocal ground between. Stalin dies and survives in East Berlin, Budapest; Churchill too, in Kenya, Malaya, Suez, Nyasaland. Perceptions of class are splintered into new formations: property-owning democracies, private affluence, floating voters. Macmillanite Toryism cleans up; Gaitskell's Labour Party dwindles in the search for the declassed middle ground and l'homme moyen …

Post Office. Late afternoon. Dunn stands by an untended grille, reading the room. Out of shot, an old man reads to someone, over slow pan of the place.

OLD MAN: *(over)* … 'The fight for peace was surrendered to the Tories. Macmillan was able to pose as the champion of the Summit and of understanding with the Soviet Union. Labour did not reply by exposing Tory policy on West German rearmament, NATO, the Cold War, the arms race and the insane policy of using the H-bomb first. On all these issues the Labour leaders declared their agreement with the Tories. Labour's policy boiled down to the claim that they would run capitalism better than the capitalists. It is not surprising that many electors should draw the conclusion that in that case the job could well be left to the party of the capitalists – the Tories ...'

The shot's reached the old pensioner and his wife. The woman fills out a form; the man reads to her from his Daily Worker. Dunn watches, listens, in the vacancy of the room.

MAN: ... That's what <u>my</u> paper says anyway.

WOMAN: I don't know why you buy that thing.

MAN: I buy it because it gives another point of view.

WOMAN: Aye, I know. Russia's.

MAN: Don't start on Russia ...

WOMAN: ... I'm not ...

MAN: ... We wouldn't be 'ere if it 'adn't bin fer Russia ...

WOMAN: *(firming up)* ... An' don't you either.

Silence. Starlings click beyond the high street window. Close shot of Dunn watching the pair.

MAN: *(finally, not quite quenched)* Wharrabout <u>your</u> paper, hunh?

WOMAN: *(minatory)* Harold ...

Silence again, still on Dunn's face.

MAN: *(disgusted but sotto)* ... Bloody Daily Express ...

VOICE: *(over, behind grille)* Jack Dunn, poste restante, Wolverton ... Aye, I thought we had someat ...

Dunn swings round. The assistant's returned, a letter in his hand.

ASSISTANT: I shall need some means of erm ...

Dunn hands him his dole card, stoops to sign for the letter. The assistant studies the card.

ASSISTANT: Long way from home, aren't we ...?

DUNN: *(Taking letter)* Aye. Walkin' holiday.

Dunn heads for the door. The old man sits alone, his wife at the counter.

DUNN: You wouldna finished wi' that, would you?

The old man frowns, looks down at his Daily Worker, begins to fold it with gnarled fingers.

MAN: Tek it. I'm finished.

Dunn takes it, thanks him, leaves. The shot closes in on the ancient's face. He speaks, gesturally to camera, tonally to himself.

MAN: My grandfather fought at Waterloo against Napoleon. And the Russians were on our side then too, by God. I'm drawin' 'is pension …

He chuckles. Mix through to

Early evening. Ellen washes her hair, waist deep in a river.

Evening. River meadow. Dunn sits outside a small patched and grubby double-tent, tending the pan of supper on the primus and scanning Ellen's sketch-pad. He's stopped on a drawing of Gyp, a quite dense pencil-portrait of head and face, a suggestion of Billy's head in the background. Moves on, less interested, through others: turns back a page, to check something. Stares at it, frowning.

ELLEN: *(Approaching,)* … You're back. Any luck?

Dunn closes the pad; watches her approach across the meadow, a towel to her hair. He holds up the opened poste restante letter.

DUNN: Cowley on the 17th. *(Shows her the map)* We're in good time.

ELLEN: Good. I'm hungry.

DUNN: Ready when you are.

She stoops, enters the tent. Dunn stirs the grub; folds map and letter into his pocket; reopens the sketch-pad.

ELLEN: *(from tent)* Any more on the Scots lads?

Close shot of the sketch he's returned to: Phelan stares along the bar of a country inn, telephone to ear.

DUNN: *(over)* Uhunh.

Cut to

The low shot gazes down an empty stretch of narrow country road, on the northern edge of Oxfordshire. Fade up sounds of approaching marchers: feet, talk, song, march chants. The column breaks into shot past the camera, three abreast, anti-nuclear flags aloft, ban-banners prominent, shepherded by the police. Jack Dunn and Ellen Pearson are glimpsed, under trade union banners: Miners Against the Bomb; For a Sane and Safe Energy Policy.

Sound fades; marchers fade; Dunn and Pearson are left, headed on. As they shrink in the distance, a huge furniture removal truck glides mutely into shot, headed after them.

Cut to reverse angle: the marchers approach camera, the pantechnicon gaining on them. Fade up sounds.

Dunn draws Ellen towards the hedgerow to let it through. The truck rumbles menacingly by, close enough to touch. The marchers resume the road; head on. Out of shot, some distance away, the truck stops. Dunn's face, on the walk, squinting down the road; Ellen's. The truck begins a slow rumbling reverse in their direction. They stop; watch. The truck stops. The vehicle's 20 feet away, wholly blocking their path.

Silence. They watch. A sudden snapping rumble, the back rolls upwards, opened from within. Gypsy Armstrong stands inside the vast space, hand on Billy's bridle, the cart looming beyond.

They stare at him; blink. Gyp smiles.

GYP: Aye. Knew ah'd bloody find ye … *(calling to driver)* Here'll do nicely, Jackie …

The driver appears round the van, releases the flap. Gyp walks the pony onto the tarmac.

GYP: … Jackie Milburn, T & G now, one time pitman up at Seaham …

Hands are shaken.

MILBURN: *(A Geordie)* Aye. Doon among the fishes … You want this thing out?

GYP: Aye, ah'll give you a hand …

ELLEN: … I'll do it.

She moves forward to help. Gives Gyp a hug as she passes. He's pleased. Looks at Jack.

GYP: *(Grinning)* … Jackie had a pick-up in Cowley, ah couldn't resist …

DUNN: How's Perce?

GYP: Day after tomorrow, all bein' well. They can't wait to get shut of him, havoc he's causin' …

DUNN: Did they …? *(His hand touches his chest)*

GYP: Wouldn't let 'em. Says e's not ready for the knacker's yard just yet … *(Pause. To the unanswered question)* E'll tek a few days to mek 'is mind up …

Dunn nods. Silence. The cart's all but down.

DUNN: What about the lass, Gyp?

GYP: *(Reaching for the pony)* Aye. Give us me marchin' orders … Ah musta started mopin' 'r someat, told us to piss off after ye … *(He grins, ruffles Billy's ears)* Say 'ello to your uncle Jack, where's your manners, man …

Dunn reaches out for the pony's head; strokes an ear.

DUNN: *(Eventually)* Right. Let's away.

Mute shot of sun setting beyond concrete bridge. Marchers, horse and cart glide blackly across the bridge, etchings on the sun; clear frame. Sound up, slow pan down onto a motorway dense with evening traffic already on headlamps.

Black.

Their march through the sixties and into the seventies, terse images cut to rock. Elements include: mods on lambrettas, death of the Herald, mugshots of Macmillan, Wilson, Heath; rising graph of unemployment, steady shrinkage of coal industry (Reprise: God's dead, love. So's mining), In Place of Strife; Cuba, Kennedy, Vietnam, Czechoslovakia; '68; hippies, flowers, powers. Fading to black.

Black. Over:

DUNN'S JOURNAL VOICE: Fifty eight days down the long road through England. Bad dream last night. Old Percy … went home. Nobody says so, but we all stand in need of the company and comradeship the Welsh lads will provide after Oxford …

Mute dreamlike shots of Oxford colleges, cut with sky-backed images of the three as they march through the town. A lone boy chorister's voice covers the centuries of privilege:

> Happy land! happy land!
> Thy fame resounds from shore to shore;

Happy land! where tis a crime
They tell us to be poor.
If you shelter cannot find,
Of you they'll soon take care: Most likely send you to grind wind
For sleeping in the air.
Happy land! happy land!
To praise thee who will cease?
To guard us, pray, now ain't we got
A precious new police?
A passport we shall soon require
Which by them must be scanned,
If we to take a walk desire –
Oh, ain't this happy land?

(Happy Land, *from* A Touch on the Times, *Penguin*)

Music dies, as a Radio One newscast takes over, on slow circling pan down to the grass quad of Ruskin, where the three wait by the march-cart in evening silence. Gyp feeds Billy from a bucket; Ellen sits by a wheel, sketching; Dunn stands impassive. The newscast centres principally on the miners' strike of '74, the picketing of coal stocks and power stations. Fades. Bring up sounds of the quad.

A man arrives, short, stocky, late 30s, from the gate area; addresses them en route, deep Pontypridd.

MAN: Jack Dunn, is it? Mike Roberts, Cardiff Organiser, you got my letter, then, eh? Welcome, comrades. *(Hands are shaken, names exchanged. Roberts smiles quizically at Ellen's presence)* … Here's the thing, see … half our boys headed off for London yesterday, rest of us've been detailed to help the Midlands lads picket the power stations, we're doin' Didcot. We've got you digs for the night, if you step out tomorrow you could catch the boys up, there's a few veterans along, you know … slows things down.

He checks his watch. Dunn looks at the others; feels the dejection.

DUNN: No chancea stayin' by a few days an' helpin' wi' the picket …?

ROBERTS: Be fine by me, brother. But your orders are to push on. That's official, see. All sections numberin' less than a dozen gotta head for London … OK –

He checks the time again. Dunn deals with the news, impassive.

ROBERTS: Listen, I got a support meetin' over in Cowley … This is one we can win, comrades. An' wi' this under our belts, we might be ready for a big un … *(Hands Dunn an envelope)* There's your digs, anything you need I've left our number …

DUNN: Thanks. *(They smile)* Good luck, comrade.

ROBERTS: You an' all. See you London, is it?

He waves to the others, bowlegs off towards the arch, one with his purpose. Dunn picks up his roll-bag, throws it on to the cart.

GYP: Shit.

Dunn nods. Ellen collects her rucksack from the grass, pouches her sketchpad, places the bag in the cart.

ROBERTS: *(Stopped; turned)* Oh aye, any word on the Irishman, since he did the bunk …?

Silence. Dunn feels Ellen's eyes on him.

DUNN: *(Distinct)* No. Nothing.

ROBERTS: Bastard probly crawled back under his stone …

He's gone. Dunn opens the envelope, studies the address inside. Ellen's eyes work on the men's faces. The sun's gone: they stand in shadow.

ELLEN: *(Eventually)* What's going on? *(Gyp shrugs, in the dark, frowns in Dunn's direction)* Jack?

Dunn pockets the letter, returns the cart's flap to its bolt.

DUNN: *(Factual)* National Union lawyers've bin talkin' to the Scots lads in Durham gaol. Word has it it was Phelan led 'em into the police ambush …

Silence. Gyp curses, low, intense.

ELLEN: D'you believe it?

DUNN: *(Slow)* It's possible.

ELLEN: How long've you known?

DUNN: Coupla weeks.

He takes out the distinctive poste-restante letter; she takes it; reads; refolds it.

ELLEN: Why didn't you tell me?

DUNN: Time to tell ye's when ah know it's true, lass. *(Pause)* 'Sides, ye've enough on yer plate …

She hands him the letter, climbs the wheel, tugs her sack from the cart.

ELLEN: OK. Where are we stopping?

DUNN: Headington Hall, it's over …

ELLEN: … I'll find it.

She walks off quite rapidly towards the entrance to the building. Gyp takes the poste-restante letter from Dunn's hands.

GYP: *(As he reads)* Where's she goin' then?

Dunn watches her disappear into the college.

DUNN: *(Bleak)* She'll be lookin' for the Irishman. He reckoned he was studyin' here …

GYP: Let's join her, get the bastard …

DUNN: Forget it, Gyp. *(A moment of stand-off. Gyp takes the meaning)* She'll do it … Come on.

High shot of the couple, leading Billy and the cart off into the street beyond. Over this, voices from the miners' strikes of the seventies discourse on their experience of police, picketing and surveillance.

Mix to

Night. Oxford streets. Ellen takes direction from a group of half-pissed student gentry, strides away from them, white-faced.

Small 18th century warren of student houses. Ellen checks an address on the paper she carries, reaches the house, goes in through communal front door, takes stairs to an upper floor.

Landing. Ellen knocks at a door, a man's voice calls her in, she enters the flat.

Ellen makes her way into the bag-strewn room, takes in the political posters round the walls: Mao, Che, Fidel, Ho, Connolly. A tv set carries a late news round-up of countrywide disruption from the continuing miners' strike.

MAN'S VOICE: *(Rear room)* You're early … I'll be a few minutes yet …

She says nothing. Fingers the family pics on the table: Phelan, his parents, brothers and sister.

Phelan in, mid-sentence, a crate of books in his hands, hair on shoulders, Villa moustache, sweat shirt, flared blue jeans.

PHELAN: … Listen, it's good of you to take this lot, I'll give you an address as soon as I have one … *(Sees her)* myself.

Silence. They stare at each other. Across the town somewhere, the remorseless whine of a police siren, lifting, dying.

PHELAN: Jesus God, it's you. *(She says nothing)* I've a mate callin' to take this lot, I'm leavin' tomorrow …

He cuts the tv.

ELLEN: Still running, Michael?

PHELAN: Maybe. You still marching?

ELLEN: Aye.

PHELAN: Sound like Jack. How are they?

ELLEN: Fine.

PHELAN: Sit down.

ELLEN: Is it true?

PHELAN: Probably.

ELLEN: You working for the police.

The doorbell rings. Neither moves.

PHELAN: Yes. *(Silence)* Do I go on? *(She nods whitely. The bell rings again)* I'll be a minute …

He leaves the flat. She's left with the room: posters, paintings, family pics, her pencil self-portrait torn from the pad and pinned to the wall. The siren again, closing. Over,

GYP'S VOICE: *(Reading, slow, stubborn)* … The modern individual family is founded on the open or concealed slavery of the wife …

Mix to

Night. Darkish brick-walled student's room in Headington Hall (Ruskin's '60s residential buildings). Dunn replaits Gypsy's washed pigtail. The hewer sups canned beer, reads from a paperback edition of The Female Eunuch.

GYP: *(On)* Within the family, he is the bourgeois and his wife represents the proletariat … Freedritch Angels, The Origin of the Family, 1843, page 79. What ye think?

DUNN: Sounds about right.

GYP: Aye?

Silence, as he thinks. The police siren continues, less distant, joined by a second.

GYP: Bloody 'ell. If it's not one thing it's another …

DUNN: *(Grinning)* Aye.

Silence again. Gyp sups on his can.

GYP: Ye think she'll find 'im, the lass?

DUNN: If he's here.

GYP: Think she'll come back?

DUNN: *(Tired suddenly)* Come back? *(Long pause)* I don't know.

Gyp drinks; Jack plaits. The siren calls on, fading.

PHELAN'S VOICE: *(Over, trailed; cold, remote)* … So there it was, the choice, clinical and clear. A sick old Republican, fitted up with a robbery charge they freely acknowledged they knew he couldn't have done, me old da', would end his days in that gaol unless I agreed to co-operate …

Cut to

Night. Lamplit bridge over the Isis. We see their hazed image on the water as they lean against the parapet, talk.

PHELAN: I said I wanted to see him. They even paid my ticket across. I thought I might … ask him what I should do, but he got in first, he said: I don't mind dyin' here, so long as I'm allowed to do it with honour … And he looked at me, you know. *(Long silence. Slow mix through to Phelan on the bridge, Ellen watching him carefully)* *(Metallic)* So. I came back. And agreed to do their doing. It was me betrayed the Scots lads up there. I did what they asked.

ELLEN: And since?

PHELAN: *(Almost angry)* No. Jesus, no. Wasn't once enough?

ELLEN: I don't know, Michael. You wouldn't say …

PHELAN: … After Tow Law, after the experience of you … and the others, the march … I thought I might top myself, you know … I saw quite clearly, quite clearly, I wasn't helpin' him, I was dishonouring him … But they kept coming and coming, all the way down, and …

He stops, thread snapped in the struggle for control. She watches him in lamplit profile; lays a warm hand on his wrist. He looks at it slowly, disbelievingly. Tears pulse unnoticed down his face.

ELLEN: And where do you go now?

PHELAN: London, I don't know. Make some money, go … home …

ELLEN: *(Soft)* We're going to London.

He shakes his head. Stares down at the water again. Slow mix to their reflection. The police siren again, closer.

PHELAN: *(Slow)* I couldn't, love. They wouldn't have me.

ELLEN: *(Eventually)* Wouldn't they? How do you know?

Slow mix to

Morning. Grounds, Headington Hall. Church bells carol the bright day. Dunn stands by Billy's head, checks his watch against the height of the sun; sees Gyp appear from the dormitory buildings. Gyp shakes his head, arriving; Dunn's lips purse for thought.

GYP: Out all night. No sign of her.

Dunn strokes the pony's nose a moment, humps his bag into the cart. A clock begins to strike: ten.

DUNN: Mebbe she made a choice, Gyp. *(Gyp screws up his face, resisting it)* We're due in London, let's go.

GYP: She'll be here, man. Ten minutes.

Bells and clock stop together; birds faintly invade the quiet. Close shots of the two men; wind ruffles Dunn's lengthened hair; Gyp rolls his earring, finger and thumb.

Day. Long country lane, college spires in remote distance. Two men, pony, cart advance mutely into the shot. Over:

DUNN: *(Journal voice)* Will Daly, Percy Mann, the Irishman: casualties of the road. And now the lass … Pray God the rest have fared better or we'll prove the sorriest huddle ever seen on Parliament Hill …

Bring up country lane sounds; marchers' feet, Billy's, the whack and bumble of the cart bleed in on their approach.

They stop. Stare in silence, held by the watcher ahead. Reverse reveals Ellen Pearson, bag on shoulder, blocking their way.

DUNN: *(Eventually)* You find him? *(She nods, quite terse)* Did he do it? *(She nods again)* And?

ELLEN: He wants to explain ...

She looks towards the trees. Phelan emerges, bag in hand; tentatively approaches the group in the lane.

GYP: Is it right, ye shopped the Scots lads ...?

PHELAN: ... It is, aye.

Gyp advances deliberately, smacks him to the ground with a single blow. Cut to

Binocular shot of the scene from half a mile away across country. Radio 1 plays close by on car radio. The man behind the glasses describes events laconically to someone nearby.

Over:

MAN'S VOICE: ... Wait on, the buggers're fightin', our Gyppo's clocked the paddy ... Nah, 'e won't fight, lilylivered fucker ...

SECOND MAN'S VOICE: ... What they doin' now ...?

MAN'S VOICE: ... Talkin', yap yap yap ...

The action continues mutely through the glasses, as music gives way to midday newscast on the radio. An election's been called: the miners are meeting to call off the action. Cut to

The lane; the group. Phelan's mouth's cut, bleeding.

ELLEN: *(On burn)* ... You're *pathetic,* all of you ... All right, he betrayed us, he betrayed his people, but the lesson's been learnt, damn you, and he's *here*, asking, asking ... he doesn't need your anger, he needs your intelligence and your understanding ... Jesus.

She takes a tissue from her pocket, offers it to Phelan, who shakes his head. Dunn's eyes search Phelan's face for dependable truths; Gyp works his bruised knuckles frowningly.

GYP: Informers're worse than scabs, Ellen, and both're worse than cancer ...

ELLEN: *(Distinct)* Yes, I know, Gyp. But people do get better ...

GYP: Nah, listen man ...

ELLEN: Don't man me, all right ...?

DUNN: *(Sharp; cutting through)* All right. *(He paces forward, faces Phelan)* What do you want, Michael?

PHELAN: *(Slow)* I want to make my peace with you, Jack. I want the chance to be a comrade again.

Dunn's eyes search on. Phelan's look is level, open, prepared for rejection. Dunn takes out a handkerchief, hands it to Phelan. He takes it; dabs the bloodied mouth.

DUNN: I'm sorry for your father, but what you did was wrong. Do you see that?

PHELAN: Yes. Very clearly.

DUNN: *(To Ellen; not a question; calm)* And you're saying we can trust him now …

ELLEN: Right.

DUNN: You sayin' anythin' else? Like, if he doesn't come, neither do you …?

Ellen closes her eyes, opens them, head shaking; takes a pace or two to close on him.

ELLEN: This is my march, Jack, just as much as yours. And I'll see it through, with or without the lot of you if I have to …

Silence. Dunn smiles, tinily. Silence. Cut to

Slow zooming pan across fields towards a huge furniture van parked in a meadow. Atop it, a man in cavalry twills, check shirt and gilet stands on binocular watch. A second man sits in the driving seat, talking on police radio frequency, sput and sizzle.

BINOCULAR MAN: *(Over, hard cockney)* … OK, looks as if they're on the move again, Bertie boy. Irishman too, well well well … Little bastard thinks 'e's given us the slip, little bastard does …

He climbs down the side of the lorry, joins his oppo in the front. The shot pulls away, reveals the sign on its side: Wilson & Co., Light Removals. *Fade to black.*

Evening. High Street, on the long western straggle to London. Late shoppers, some bustle and fume. Jack, Ellen and Phelan watch a bank of mute TV screens through a Dixons window. On the screens, wrapped in the New Giant Blue of the New Tory Logo, Thatcher Mk 1 acknowledges the mounting fervour of the Conference's standing ovation. The three watch in silence, as if ghosts; as if not there.

At the curb, Gyp waits with Billy, the cart gone. He talks as he stares watchfully up the High Street; feeds him carrots from a paper bag.

GYP: ... Look, ahm tellin' ye, man, it'll be like a rest 'ome, Barney's a good un, Gateshead lad, came down after the war, he'll look after ye, he's offering a field to yoursel' an' fodder for life, you get your feet up, son, God knows you've earned it ... (*He reaches down to feel the pony's swollen fetlocks, Billy backs gingerly away)*It's for the best, Bill. You've pulled your weight, tell 'em ...

He checks out the three windowgazers, resumes his watch. Thinks he sees what he's looking for, whistles the three to look. A tall transporter truck – perhaps a horse box – noses down the street, draws up by the next corner.

DUNN: *(Heading in)* That him, d'ye think?

GYP: I reckon, the dozy bugger ... *(Hands Jack Billy's lead rope)* I'll tek a look.

Gyp heads for the truck, the others in his wake. Ellen and Phelan take Billy from Dunn, begin to say their goodbyes as they lead him towards the waiting pantechnicon.

Gyp, approaching the unmarked truck. His face, a slight frown forming. The shot angles up to take in the high cabin: it's empty.

GYP: *(calling to them as they reach the rear)* Don't think it's 'im. False alarm ...

He steps up onto the running board to peer into the cabin. The truck explodes. Smoke, flame, glass, screams, shouts, sirens, silence, moans, calls.

Slow hovering track of the pavement; bodies, glass, rubble, the randomly scattered contents of store windows loom ghost-like from the thick hang of smoke. Through it all, the Tory Conference standing ovation continues. Sirens, closing. The shot reaches Dunn, crumpled, lifeless, bloodied. Holds. His eyes open suddenly, see nothing, close. Bleed in local radio beeps and news headlines: Terror bomb in High Street, two dead, twenty injured; inner-city riots, third day; unemployment 2.5million, thousands join the March for Jobs ... .

Shuttered room, strong sunlight from outside; in feel, somewhere between country house and cottage hospital. A whitecoated man sits at the bottom of an ironframe bed, making notes on a clip pad. Local radio returns to music in a room nearby. Sounds from the bed. The man looks up. His view of the bed: Dunn stirs uneasily, head bandaged, eyelids flickering. The man gathers his phone, calls someone.

MAN: *(phone)* Coming to. Ahunh. Will do.

Dunn struggles to sit, dizzies, manages.

DUNN: Where's this?

MAN: *(a smile)* You're a very fortunate man, Mr Dunn. Oh yes.

Dunn looks him over, takes in the phone, the room.

DUNN: Oh aye?

Cut to

Another room. A whitecoated man stands by the shuttered windows staring out through the cracks. At the bed, a nurse finishes redressing Gyp's arms and neck; eventually gathers her things and leaves. Gyp stares blankly at the shutter-lit ceiling.

MAN: *(resuming; not looking)* ... Armstrong, Daniel Palmer; aka Gypsy. Two Chapel Green, Easley. Ring any bells, Mr Armstrong ...?

He looks across at the unmoving Gyp. Gyp turns his head to take in the whitecoat.

GYP: Sorry, ye speakin' to me?

Long upper-storey corridor, shutterlit. A white-coated man pushes a robed patient towards a locked door at the far end; leaves the chair eventually, to unlock the door.

Close shot of Ellen in the chair, legs and hands bandaged. Fragments of the explosion burst again in her head. She moans her way back in to the corridor. The whitecoat returns to the wheelchair.

MAN: You're in safe hands, Mrs Pearson. Easy does it ...

He eases her through the open door and on through a second into a large, shuttered, brightly lit room. A young woman, wheelchair, robe, looks up, smiles; a nurse at her feet has almost finished redressing her leg wounds.

MAN: Mrs Pearson, Sister. Mrs Drummond's asked to see her.

The nurse nods, secures the dressing, goes out to look for him. The whitecoat takes his leave. The woman takes in Ellen's pale strained face. Offers her a polo.

WOMAN: What a carry on, eh. Josie, how d'you do. I wouldn't mind, I wasn't even in the same street. (*Shows her dressed legs and feet*) Still, I suppose we're the lucky ones ... Local, are you, family ...? (*Ellen shakes her head*) I was on my way home ... They said they'd let my husband know, he's on the rigs, Persian Gulf, but they haven't said. Are you all right, lovie ...? Are you? Listen, if you've anyone needs calling, jot down the number, I'll have my sister do it, she'll be in tonight ... (*Looks around the spare clinical room*) Ooh, I hate these places ... (*Reaches for a pad and pencil on the desk*) Here, put it here, I'll see they're called, leave it to me ...

Cut to

The two women on a black and white monitor, two men watching, making notes.

WATCHER: Good lass. Go for it girl ... Bollocks!

On screen, the two women turn as the door opens and a whitecoated woman comes in.

WATCHER: ... Fucking Drummond!

Cut to

Black and white monitor, men watching: Dunn's room.

WHITECOAT: (*On screen*) Is there someone we should get in touch with, wife, friends ...?

DUNN: Uhunh.

WHITECOAT: You left Easley around two months ago, right? What've you been doing ...?

DUNN: Looking for work.

WHITECOAT: Is that what you were doing in Reading?

DUNN: Is it your business?

WHITECOAT: We have to fill out a report ...

DUNN: Who for?

The whitecoat sniffs, sits back in his chair.

WATCHER: Enemy within. Definitely.

Cut to

Domestic tv screen: Thatcher on the Miners' Strike, late '84. Ellen and

Josie sit watching, day clothes, shuttered room. Close shot Ellen's face: images of the explosion burst again in her head; Billy; Phelan's ghastly slowmo attempt to shield her ...

JOSIE: I don't know, it's chaos everywhere you look, bombers, striking miners, riots, I can't understand it ... My Frank says if Mrs T. can't put a stop to it we'll be looking for a Mr H. *(Pause)* Hitler. It's his little joke.

Ellen blinks, moans a little, holds her middle.

JOSIE: Young man died from his wounds on Ward K this morning, did you hear? Couldn'ta been more than thirty, there was nothing left of him, poor thing ... They say he was Irish. That's what they call ironic, I'd say. You all right, lovie?

Ellen stares at her, face gripped with pain; shakes her head. Cut to

Monitor shot of the two women, Ellen doubling with pain, Josie comforting her, beginning to call for help.

WATCHER: *(voice over; his shadow on the screen)* Better get the Duty MO over there pronto, James, or we could be losing another of the buggers ...

Cut to

Shuttered office. Dunn, head lightly bandaged, sits facing an interview desk, an empty chair beyond it. He studies a typed statement on the desk, a pen beside it. Eventually lays it down. Stands. Gives the room a long slow searching scan. Stops at something beyond the curtain rail. Cut to

Monitor screen. Dunn's face stares up at the lens. In the background somewhere, radio news covers the miners' return to work (March '85).

WATCHER: *(voice over)* Ohu. Let Cherry know before he goes in, the bugger's found us ...

Office. Dunn returns to his chair. The door opens. A whitecoat takes the empty chair, scans the unsigned statement, stares at Dunn across the desk. Dunn takes his look, then stares deliberately at the hidden lens.

WHITECOAT: Yes yes, you've located the camera, a man of your experience, you're bound to have an edge ... *(Removes white coat)* Believe it or not, it's for your own protection, ensures we don't overstep the mark in our zeal to put the bloody murderers away for the rest of their miserable lives ...

DUNN: ... We?

WHITECOAT: What?

DUNN: You said we, who's we ...?

WHITECOAT: We're the state, Mr Dunn. Or is that comrade? We defend the
realm. Against scum like yourself. Shall we get on? *(He flicks the
statement across the desk)* There's nothing there we can't back up with
hard evidence, Dunn, you were there at the lorry with your three co-
conspirators, that's ... *(Checks pad)* ... Armstrong, the woman
Pearson and our friend Phelan, all right? Just sign at the bottom and
we can wrap the thing up. Friend Phelan's dead, by the way, so if you
want to lay most of it on him that's fine by us, but we need your
signature, OK?*(Hands him the pen)* Shall we?

DUNN: What about the others?

WHITECOAT: They're in good hands. They're giving us all we need,
Armstrong especially, the female comrade was carrying, did you know?

DUNN: Was?

WHITECOAT: *(A smile)* Lost it this morning. There you go. But she'll talk
soon enough, once she knows what we have ... She's given us a lead
already, we've had her mother brought in, I believe you all put up at
her house a couple of weeks back ...

DUNN: Do you get paid for this? You should be doing fiction. I'd like to
leave this place now, I've better things to do than listen to this crap ...

WHITECOAT: Just sign the statement, boy. Then we'll see.

*Dunn breathes deep, stretches, reaches for the pen, signs. The Man
smiles, takes the paper, reads the signature, sniffs, crumples the paper,
takes out a copy, pushes it back at Dunn.*

WHITECOAT: I think you're going to have to sign your own name,
sunshine, we've got Mickey Mouse inside already ...

DUNN: Sorry. Best I can do.

WHITECOAT: We'll see. Maybe it's escaped your notice in your hectic dash
to change the world, friend, but we're running the show now, not
scumbags like you and your murderous mates ... Think it over.

*He smiles again, gets up, leaves. Dunn sits on, gazing at the statement.
The door opens, a whitecoated man beckons him with a crooked
forefinger. Cut to*

Long shuttered corridor. The Whitecoat stands Dunn by while he opens a locked door. Dunn peers out through a crack in the shutter. Looks down on a small 18th century walled garden. Sees a familiar figure in a wheelchair being interviewed by a whitecoat. Cut to

Garden. Day. Gyp sits at a garden table watching a bunch of blackbirds vying for feeding space with a gang of thrushes on the small polished lawn. The Whitecoat sits opposite, talking, making notes.

WHITECOAT: ... There's more, much more, Mr Armstrong. There's twenty years of subversion in the dossier, strikes, marches, demonstrations, sit-ins, so-called Anti-Nazi League, peace demos, anti-poll tax shenanigans, it's all there friend, we've logged your every fart and belch for years, so make no mistake, we'll wear you down, whether you sign or not ... You hearing me?

GYP: S'funny, I thought this were a hospital.

WHITECOAT: S'a private clinic.

GYP: Private clinic. Mmm. What can I say, I've lost me memory. I don't know nothin' ...

WHITECOAT: Yesterday you remembered your mother, man ...

GYP: Did ah? Ah don't remember ...

A car siren sounds, closing, beyond the wall.

WHITECOAT: What about the pony? Do you remember the pony? *(Close shot, Gyp's face, paying no heed)* What did you call him, Billy was it? *(Gyp's face again: nothing)* Blown to buggery anyway. He'll be Whiskas by now ...

A second Whitecoat unlocks a gate, hurries across to the table, stoops to mutter something into his colleague's ear. The guy nods, the man leaves. Gyp stares on at the squabble of birds.

WHITECOAT: Well, your luck may be in after all, Gyppo. The lads have brought in another vanload of meat for processing ... Seems you could be off the hook. For the moment.

Gyp looks at him carefully.

GYP: What is this place?

WHITECOAT: *(A smile)* This? This is England.

He stands, saunters off. Close shot, Gyp's face, dealing with Billy.

Van, on the move; night. The three sit in silence in the near-dark, facing their three guards. The van radio filters back through the grille: a news report deals with the second ballot for the Tory leadership; a second item covers the new pit closure programme ...

The van slows; stops. Doors bang. Footsteps. The rear doors are opened, a guard nods curtly to the three, who clamber down into the darkness.

They stand to watch the van move off into the night. For a long moment they are nowhere, until one by one the street lights come on.

They stare in silence at the deserted High Street from earlier. Like ghosts, they begin to walk it, through the rot and rubbish of a post-eighties British city ...

Fade to black.

Fade up streets approaching Parliament Hill, day faded, filled with people, purposeful, quiet, on the move. Ahead, a mile or so, the steady surge and lap of a large gathering.

A touch darker. Grassy approaches to the hill itself, lit by slung lamps. Marchers queue at rude tables for accreditation, hurry through, excited by the noise and light, new badges glittering in the lamplight.

Dunn reaches the table, lays out their cards for checking. Officials wave them through.

Night. The din from the hill, voices in their hundreds pulsing down the long grass slope, grows on their approach. Fires flick and leap, lamps swing in the night. Old comrades rejoin them as they begin the ascent: Albert, the Easley Lodge Chairman; Mary Dunn, her son and father; the two cowmen and their families; Will Daly, back from Nicaragua, a leg missing; Percy Mann in a wheelchair.

The shot accompanies them on the climb, glancing right and left at the contingents clustered by their fires as they go. Glimpsed rather than seen, perched precariously on hard and unyielding ground, six centuries of struggle gather on the hillside, eating, drinking, arguing, laughing, from Wat Tyler to now, Lollards, Diggers, Levellers, Republicans, Luddites, Chartists, Tolpuddle Martyrs, Suffragettes, Pacifists, on and up to the broad scatter of contemporary practice and belief. The hill smoulders with discourse, a pulsing convocation of militant voices, six hundred years of 'enemies within' articulating the vision of a post-capitalist world. Posters and flags herald the new millennium.

The group reach the brow; stare down on the sleeping capital, burning as it sleeps.

GYP: Good turn out, eh?

ELLEN: Are we there?

DUNN: There? No. But we're here.

They look again at the city. The shot pans across it. Begin credits, mixing through to

Day. Still image of long empty stretch of country lane in long shot. A figure crests a rise in the far distance, headed for camera, a rolled kit-bag on his shoulder. Bring up sounds of a six-piece pit-band tuning up. The advancing figure holds the road alone for some while, then others appear, in twos and threes, optically inserted, till the lane's dense with marching figures. The crowded way gradually thins back to the solitary marcher: it's Dunn, head cropped, eyes fierce.

———— END ————

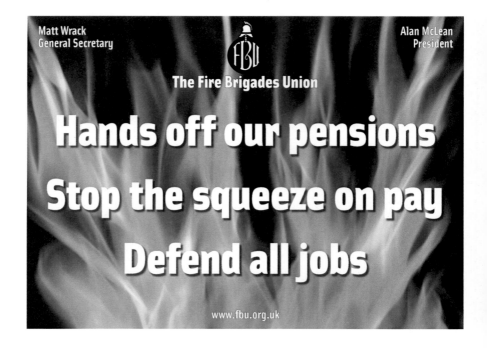

Social Security

Ruth Lister

*Ruth Lister worked for the
Child Poverty Action
Group for many years and
is now its Honorary
President. She is Emeritus
Professor of Social Policy
at Loughborough
University and her
writings include*
Citizenship: Feminist
Perspectives *(Palgrave,
2003),* Poverty *(Polity,
2004), and* Gendering
Citizenship in Western
Europe *(with F. Williams
et al, Policy Press, 2007).
Ed Miliband appointed
her to the House of Lords
in 2010.*

Having passed the Welfare Reform Act
2012, against widespread opposition, David
Cameron and his government have warned
of what they will do if they are left to their
own devices: for example, no housing
benefits for many young people, stopping
payments of child-related benefits to out of
work families with more than three
children, and time-limiting benefits for the
long-term unemployed. The stakes couldn't
be higher. How to respond?

Winning public support for spending on
benefits will not simply be a matter of some
new eye-catching policy proposals. First,
the whole debate on benefits needs re-
framing. A growing belief that poverty is
due more to individual failings than to
injustice; diminishing support for
redistribution through the tax-benefit
system; and a growing belief that benefits
are too high and discourage work incentives
and 'scrounging' appear to be undermining
any sense of solidarity with benefit
recipients. Public attitudes are mirroring
pretty consistent messages from
government (New Labour as well as the
Coalition). For some time politicians have
denounced a supposed 'dependency culture'
and irresponsible benefit claimants, while
ever more punitive rules appear to have
increased mistrust in the benefits system,
rather than allay it. The Conservative-led
government's individualistic behaviour-
based diagnosis of the causes of poverty has
triumphed in a country where public
attitudes have always been more prone to
blame 'the poor' than in continental Europe.

Public attitudes are clearly not fixed, but
that does not mean it will be easy to shift the
tide. A first step in re-framing the debate

could be to reassert a clear structural analysis of poverty and an understanding of how individual agency is constrained. Then we need to stop talking about 'welfare', which has taken on such divisive and pejorative meanings, and reclaim the language of social security or social protection. This could speak to the growing sense of insecurity felt by many citizens. We need to remind people that social security is not just about poverty relief, but also about guaranteeing a degree of economic security for everyone. This points away from such heavy reliance on means-testing, which 'others' recipients and creates resentment among some of those who do not qualify.

Evidence of the value the public attaches to reciprocity has rekindled interest in the contributory principle. A recent Touchstone pamphlet by Kate Bell and Declan Gaffney (*Making a contribution*, TUC, 2012) makes the case for strengthening contributory benefits as one (though not the only) means of addressing the crisis of public confidence in the social security system. Instead of a negative case based on attacking 'something for nothing', it considers ways of increasing the returns to contributions. Another option might be that aired by the Commission for Social Justice: allow payment of higher contributions in return for higher benefits. 'Premium' national insurance might be sold as superior to private insurance and bind more people into the scheme.

* * *

It is worth pausing to interrogate that word 'welfare'. What does it conjure up for you? The state of faring well? The institutions of the welfare state, with its promise of security for all from cradle to grave? Or a narrow, rather miserable, form of social assistance for people in poverty?

The last is the meaning imported from the United States, where it is the term used to describe means-tested financial support for people of working age. And with it came negative connotations of 'dependency' – a state that marks the universal human condition but that turned into a label stuck only on benefit claimants. The assumption that welfare creates 'dependency culture' underpins the government's reform agenda. From a common aspiration, welfare has been turned into a divisive notion that sets 'the poor' apart from the rest of society.

This American import has not only besmirched the concept of welfare, but also displaced the term 'social security'. Once upon a time, the Welfare Reform Act would have been called a social security act. New Labour, in its wisdom, deleted social security from the policy lexicon. In its place it, too, adopted the language of welfare reform, and the Department for Work and Pensions replaced the Department of Social Security.

In his first speech as secretary of state for work and pensions, in 2008, James Purnell underlined the significance of this move: 'My title ... embodies an ideological break with the past ... What a telling name: security as something handed down; welfare as bureaucratic transfer; people as recipients of funds ... The new title tells a wholly different story. It tells you that work is the best route to personal welfare and wellbeing; it tells you that if you work hard and contribute then you deserve your retirement to be free from anxiety about money.'

But what about the people for whom work does not, or even cannot, provide the route to wellbeing in either the short or longer term, or for whom there are no jobs available? Social security was established to protect their welfare or wellbeing. Yes, it may conjure up images of top-down bureaucracy – and not always an efficient or benign one at that. But social security is not simply a bureaucratic means; it also represents an end to which society aspires. It expresses the desire to ensure genuine security for all through social means. At a time of such great economic insecurity, we must not forget this fundamental protective function.

It provides protection against a range of risks that disrupt income from the labour market and it shares some of the costs associated with, for instance, disability or raising children. It not only redistributes resources from groups who need the money less to those who need it more – its Robin Hood function – but also contributes to the economic security of us all through its piggy-bank function, which helps us transfer money over the life cycle to when we need it more. Yet much of today's debate about social security ignores its wider functions because it assumes the much narrower role of the relief of poverty after the event, rather than its prevention.

The 'social' in social security recognises that private insurance cannot perform this protective function for the whole population in an equitable and efficient way. It is an expression of social solidarity – best expressed through more universal, non-means-tested mechanisms, which give genuine expression to the 'we're all in this together' principle.

In this context, it's encouraging that there is renewed interest in the contributory principle – the idea that entitlement to benefit should be linked not to means but to contributions made (or credited). We have seen proposals (not all attractive) to strengthen contributory benefits from both the right and the centre-left. For instance, from the right, Policy Exchange has floated a number of options for reinstating a link between contributions and benefit receipt: stronger conditionality for those without a contribution record; higher benefit levels for those who have made contributions; and personal welfare accounts in place of collective and redistributive national insurance. These proposals are motivated by a desire to strengthen individual self-reliance rather than social security's protective functions.

In contrast, from the centre-left, the Institute for Public Policy Research has proposed a 'national salary insurance', sub-titling its report 'Reforming the welfare state to provide real protection'. It makes the case for reviving the national insurance ideal, focusing on unemployed people who currently receive lamentably inadequate income protection compared with that in most other countries in the Organisation for Economic Co-operation and Decvelopment. A national salary insurance would provide unemployed people with up to 70 per cent of their previous earnings for up to six months, up to a maximum of £200 a week (including the existing £67.50 jobseeker's allowance). The idea is similar to the earnings-related supplement, which used to be paid on top of short term national insurance benefits and which was abolished by the first Thatcher government. There is one catch though – the additional amount would in effect be an interest free loan because it would be recouped through the national insurance system once back in work. This could be problematic, particularly for people who can find only low paid work

Both right and centre-left versions of a revitalised contributory principle are animated by the spirit of 'something for something' – that slogan beloved of politicians on both sides of the political divide. While this slogan can encourage the principle of reciprocity, all too often it has more punitive overtones. As such, it points towards a potentially more exclusive contributory benefit system.

Yet a criticism made of the national insurance system in the past was that it excluded many people such as part-time workers (mainly women) who were unable to build up a full contributions record. From this perspective, it's worth looking back at the report of the Commission on Social Justice (of which I was a member) set up by John Smith to advise the Labour party. We called for a more inclusive social insurance system better designed to reflect contemporary employment patterns. We also suggested modern social insurance could give its members the option of paying higher contributions in return for higher benefits. This would introduce an element of personalisation without sacrificing the principle of collective solidarity.

At a time of growing economic insecurity, socioeconomic division and widespread poverty, we urgently need a social security system that provides genuine security, ensures an adequate standard of living sufficient to enable people to live with dignity, and guarantees genuine welfare.

With acknowledgements to The Guardian and Fabian Review

Care and Health

Dexter Whitfield

Dexter Whitfield is the author of In Place of Austerity *(Spokesman, 2012) and Director of the European Services Strategy Unit. In this review article, he considers a recent 'drama' by Nick Timmins, who for many years reported public service policy in the* Financial Times.

Never Again is a fascinating and important account of how the Health and Social Care Act 2012 became law. It charts the twists and turns, power struggles, corporate lobbying, and activities of MPs, academics and advisers who perennially claim to act in the 'best interests' of the NHS.

The Coalition Government made a commitment to '... *stop the top-down reorganisations of the NHS*' in the programme for government in May 2010, but within weeks it had launched the biggest reorganisation of the NHS in its 63-year history, and the most significant shift in power and accountability.

Although the about-face and the scale of the reorganisation was a 'shock' to many, most of the policies in the 'Liberating the NHS' white paper had been advocated by Andrew Lansley in his six-and-a-half-year stint as shadow minister of health. Timmins shows that the commissioning board, clinically-led commissioning with GPs purchasing care, a new economic regulator, 'any willing provider', and Healthwatch had been promoted in numerous speeches and documents, but had received little media coverage prior to and during the 2010 general election.

The study is organised in five acts and scenes. It is vital to read the first act because it sets out the organisational and operational changes beginning with the Thatcher Government's 'Working for Patients' white paper, in 1989, and concluding with the Labour Governments' record under Blair and Brown.

Labour did initially abolish GP fundholding and 'total purchasing pilots', but later launched Foundation Trusts, private sector-run Independent Surgical Treatment Centres, practice-based commissioning, and required Primary Care Trusts to transfer service provision to arms length companies, social enterprises or the private sector. Later, the Brown Government floated the idea of a national commissioning board.

Timmins charts the ebb and flow of NHS policy over the 1989-2010 period, which is crucial to understanding the 2010 white paper. He describes Kenneth Clarke's 1989 proposals for the internal market and NHS Trusts as '... *while revolutionary in concept, were evolutionary in implementation*', in contrast to the 2010 white paper's 'big bang' approach.

The book's bye-line is 'a study in coalition government and policy making' and it does that admirably well. It charts the parliamentary lobbying process and exposes many of the vested interests. However, it is primarily an analysis of the process of the Health and Social Care Bill through Parliament and responses of the medical colleges. It only touches on the wider strident opposition from health campaigns, trade union and community organisations. A parallel analysis is needed of the successes/failures and strengths/weaknesses of the campaign outside Parliament. This should be a rigorous assessment to draw out the lessons learnt from the strategies, organising, coalition and alliance building, and national/local workplace, civil and community action.

Never Again concludes with ten lessons from the passage of the Act. Timmins concludes,

> 'what was missing from the entire exercise was a narrative, a definition of precisely what problem this mighty piece of legislation was meant to solve and how – done in this way and at this time – it did indeed solve it.'

Other lessons include the lack of internal challenge within the Conservative Party, the speed of the Coalition negotiations, and lack of expertise in the preparation of the programme for government, the weakness of the civil service in the face of a determined minister, and the need to be more accountable and to build support for reform measures.

The belief in competition, markets and commissioning (requiring a purchaser/provider split) has dictated the formation of NHS policy over the last three decades. The political consensus, rooted in neo-liberal ideology, inevitably means that NHS policies are merely variants with a common theme. Policies will continue to ebb and flow within the parameters of this consensus, and the degree of implementation will be determined by a power struggle between civil servants, corporate interests, NHS staff and trade unions, professional groups, patients and community organisations.

Waiting to see whether the Health and Social Care Act works, or not, is surely not relevant. It is constructed on competition and markets, so even if some elements are claimed to be 'successful', they will have marginal benefit. It is equivalent to getting a neat arrangement of deckchairs on the Titanic when it is steaming full speed towards destruction.

It is futile to say 'never again', even more so when there is no clear radical alternative for the NHS that has wide trade union and community support. The absence of an alternative vision and policies means that every policy change produced by the main political parties is judged according to how it affects the current model, and the degree to which it increases or decreases competition and market mechanisms.

The Timmins study highlights the lessons to be learnt in the approach to public service reform, the capabilities needed at the centre of government, changes in the policy making and legislative processes, and strengthening public management. Most of all it, reveals how policy is trapped in a neo-liberal framework with private sector vested interests continually increasing their power and influence.

Never Again: The story of the Health and Social Care Act 2012, by Nicholas Timmins, Institute for Government and The Kings Fund, 2012
www.instituteforgovernment.org.uk
www.european-services-strategy.org.uk

Semtex

'I am the bone to which all other bones
have bent. I am plastic. My grammar is
I will. Words wear my terrorist explosives
and I have primed a fissile tongue to fuse
religions, to make gods and oppose them other.
I chew lexicons to put the slime behind
and melt the world's solid shape. My lips stutter
sin's documentaries, tell each episode
of salvation's soap. I scream outrage
in time's unhearing amphitheatre. *I will*.
Language within a world that lacks language
moulds me the semtex architect of hell.'

From *Jolly Roger*
by Keith Howden

www.smokestackbooks.co.uk

HIROSHIMA

FREE PUBLIC EXHIBITION WITH A-BOMB ARTEFACTS

9–27 OCTOBER 2012, GASWORKS ARTS PARK, MELBOURNE

THE BERTRAND RUSSELL PEACE FOUNDATION

DOSSIER

2012   Number 118

HIROSHIMA PEACE DECLARATION

On 6 August 2012, during the World Conference against Atomic and Hydrogen Bombs, the Mayor of Hiroshima, Kazumi Matsui, issued this declaration to mark the 67th anniversary of the nuclear bombing of his City. Some related declarations follow.

8:15am, 6 August 1945. Our hometown was reduced to ashes by a single atomic bomb. The houses we came home to, our everyday lives, the customs we cherished – all were gone:

> 'Hiroshima was no more. The city had vanished. No roads, just a burnt plain of rubble as far as I could see, and, sadly, I could see too far. I followed electric lines that had fallen along what I took to be tram rails. The tram street was hot. Death was all around.'

That was our city, as seen by a young woman of twenty. That was Hiroshima for all the survivors. The exciting festivals, playing in boats, fishing and clamming, children catching long-armed shrimp – a way of life had disappeared from our beloved rivers.

Worse yet, the bomb snuffed out the sacred lives of so many human beings:

> 'I rode in a truck with a civil defence team to pick up corpses. I was just a boy, so they told me to grab the ankles. I did, but the skin slipped right off. I couldn't hold on. I steeled myself, squeezed hard with my fingertips, and the flesh started oozing. A terrible stench. I gripped right down to the bone. With a "one-two-three", we tossed them into the truck.'

As seen in the experience of this 13-year-old boy, our city had become a living hell. Countless corpses lay everywhere, piled on top of each other; amid the moans of unearthly voices, infants sucked at the breasts of dead mothers, while dazed, empty-eyed mothers clutched their dead babies.

A girl of sixteen lost her whole family, one after the other:

> 'My 7-year-old brother was burned from head to toe. He died soon after the bombing. A month later, my parents died; then, my 13-year-old brother and my 11-year-old sister. The only ones left were myself and my little brother, who was three, and he died later of cancer.'

From newborns to grandmothers, by the end of the year, 140,000 precious lives were taken from Hiroshima.

Hiroshima was plunged into deepest darkness. Our *hibakusha* experienced the bombing in flesh and blood. Then, they had to live with after-effects and social prejudice. Even so, they soon began telling the world about their experience. Transcending rage and hatred, they revealed the utter inhumanity of nuclear weapons and worked tirelessly to abolish those weapons. We want the world to know of their hardship, their grief, their pain, and their selfless desire.

The average *hibakushai* is now more than 78 years old. This summer, in response to many ordinary citizens seeking to inherit and pass on their experience and desire, Hiroshima has begun carefully training official *hibakusha* successors. Determined never to let the atomic bombing fade from memory, we intend to share with ever more people at home and abroad the *hibakusha* desire for a nuclear-weapons-free world.

People of the world! Especially the leaders of nuclear-armed nations, please come to Hiroshima and contemplate peace in this A-bombed city.

This year, Mayors for Peace marked its 30th anniversary. The number of cities calling for the total abolition of nuclear weapons by 2020 has passed 5,300, and our members now represent approximately a billion people. Next August, we will hold a Mayors for Peace general conference in Hiroshima. That event will convey to the world the intense desire of the overwhelming majority of our citizens for a nuclear weapons convention and elimination of nuclear weapons. The following spring, Hiroshima will host a ministerial meeting of the Non-Proliferation and Disarmament Initiative comprising ten non-nuclear-weapons states, including Japan. I firmly believe that the demand for freedom from nuclear weapons will soon spread out from Hiroshima, encircle the globe, and lead us to genuine world peace.

March 11, 2011 was a day we will never forget. A natural disaster compounded by a nuclear power accident created an unprecedented catastrophe. Here in Hiroshima, we are keenly aware that the survivors of that catastrophe still suffer terribly, yet look towards the future with hope. We see their ordeal clearly superimposed on what we endured 67 years ago. I speak now to all the stricken areas. Please hold fast to your hope for tomorrow. Your day will arrive, absolutely. Our hearts are with you.

Having learned a lesson from that horrific accident, Japan is now engaged in a national debate over its energy policy, with some voices insisting 'nuclear energy and humankind cannot coexist'. I call on the Japanese government to establish, without delay, an energy policy that guards the safety and security of the people. I ask the government of the only country to experience an atomic bombing to accept as its own the resolve of Hiroshima and Nagasaki. Mindful of the unstable situation surrounding us in North-east Asia, please display bolder leadership in the movement to eliminate nuclear weapons. Please also provide more caring measures for the *hibakusha* inside and outside Japan who still suffer even today, and take the political decision to expand the 'black rain areas'.

Once again, we offer our heartfelt prayers for the peaceful repose of the atomic bomb victims. From our base here in Hiroshima, we pledge to convey to the world the experience and desire of our *hibakusha*, and do everything in our power to achieve the genuine peace of a world without nuclear weapons.

*   *   *

20th World Congress
From Hiroshima to Future Generations
International Physicians for the Prevention of Nuclear War
Hiroshima, Japan, 24 August 2012

On the historic occasion of IPPNW's 20th World Congress, we are witnessing a sea change in global demand for a world free of nuclear weapons and free of the threat they pose to human survival. An emergent movement focused on the catastrophic humanitarian consequences of nuclear weapons is bringing States and civil society together as partners in working for a global treaty to ban and eliminate the most abhorrent weapons ever created.

We are equally encouraged by the growing demand for action to arrest the global crisis of armed violence that kills hundreds of thousands of people and maims millions more every year in countries around the world. The prevention of war is a public health imperative that extends from the carnage inflicted by small arms and light weapons to the extinction of humanity itself in a nuclear war. These signs of change are cause for hope that the international community can create a healthier, more peaceful future, where human security is based upon mutual respect and co-operation rather than the force of arms.

We rededicate ourselves to this most urgent task in Hiroshima, the first of the two Japanese cities destroyed by the bomb and rebuilt as global emissaries of peace. We honour the *Hibakusha* of Hiroshima and Nagasaki, and thank them for bringing their personal stories of suffering and survival to the rest of the world in the effort to ensure that no one else dies in a nuclear firestorm, or from the radiation that makes nuclear weapons unique and merciless in their effects.

We welcome the Peace Declaration issued by Mayor Matsui on August 6, in which he observed that Mayors For Peace, on its 30th anniversary, has now enrolled more than 5,300 municipal officials who have joined in a universal appeal for what he has called 'the genuine peace of a world without nuclear weapons'. We congratulate Mayor Taue of Nagasaki for opening a Research Centre for Nuclear Weapons Abolition at Nagasaki University, and echo his call for a nuclear weapons convention. We declare our intent to stand with Mayor Matsui, Mayor Taue, and the *Hibakusha* of both cities until we have achieved our common goal.

For more than three decades, IPPNW has endeavoured to alert health professionals, political leaders, and the public about the health effects of nuclear warfare. Most recently, IPPNW, working with its US affiliate, Physicians for Social Responsibility, and prominent climate scientists, has published important new scientific findings about the global climate disruption and devastating crop failures that would result from a nuclear war using even a fraction of the world's current arsenals. Beyond the instantaneous destruction of entire cities and the immediate deaths of tens of millions of people, the 'nuclear famine' that would persist for a decade or more could take the lives of at least a billion people in places far removed from the bombs and those who decided to use them.

We are therefore especially encouraged by the resurgence of diplomatic and governmental attention to the catastrophic humanitarian consequences of nuclear weapons and to the medical and moral imperative for nuclear disarmament. A 16-nation statement on the humanitarian basis for nuclear disarmament, issued at the 2012 Nuclear Non-Proliferation Treaty PrepCom in Vienna, has become the basis for an international conference, to be held in Oslo next March, to focus world attention on the humanitarian dangers posed by nuclear weapons. We have given this conference our unconditional support, and believe it can lay the foundation for an international treaty that will finally rid the world of nuclear weapons.

IPPNW attaches special importance to the renewed resolve of the International Red Cross and Red Crescent movement to prevent 'the unspeakable human suffering' caused by nuclear weapons; to ensure that they are never used again; and to take 'concrete actions leading to the prohibition of use and elimination of such weapons'. The Red Cross has repeatedly warned that any nuclear war, anywhere in the world, would overwhelm any possible medical response. IPPNW and the Red Cross and Red Crescent movement are of one mind about the need to abolish nuclear weapons and to prevent them from ever being used again. Therefore, we are delighted that Red Cross and Red Crescent representatives, including Federation President Tadateru Konoe, have joined us in Hiroshima.

ICAN – the International Campaign to Abolish Nuclear Weapons – is mobilizing public support for a nuclear weapons convention, an idea championed by Secretary-General Ban Ki-moon, Desmond Tutu and other prominent leaders. ICAN, launched by IPPNW in 2007, has now grown into a broad-based, multinational civil society campaign in which we are proud to be the lead medical voice as well as the founding partner organization.

IPPNW doctors, researchers, and activists also serve as the public health voice of the civil society campaigns to end the use of cluster munitions, prevent illegal global arms trade, and address the root causes of armed violence. Through our Aiming For Prevention programme, we have put human faces on the world's failure to invest in community violence prevention initiatives, and to confront a system of global gun trafficking that destroys not only individual lives and livelihoods, but also families and entire communities. At the recently – and disappointingly – concluded Arms Trade Treaty Diplomatic Conference, IPPNW presented a Medical Alert for a Strong and Humanitarian ATT, containing the signatures of thousands of health professionals from 58 countries, to Secretary-General Ban Ki-moon. We renew our call for a global agreement to ensure that conventional weapons do not end up in the hands of those who use them deliberately and indiscriminately against civilian populations or to violate anyone's human rights.

As we gather in Japan – the only country against which nuclear weapons have been used in acts of war – for the purpose of rededicating ourselves to their abolition and to the prevention of armed violence, we must also remember the tragic events at Fukushima from which the people of this country are still suffering 18 months later. The entire nuclear chain – including uranium mining and processing, the production of energy from fissionable materials in dangerous reactors, contamination from nuclear waste products, and nuclear weapons themselves – is fraught with risks to health, our environment, and our security, and we must take action to prevent future harm of such magnitude. At the same time, for more than half a century nuclear weapons have been the greatest menace to our health and survival at every stage of their development, manufacturing, testing, and use. We renew our resolve to care for the health of the global *Hibakusha*, learning from the expertise in radiation medicine and radiation protection gained from the precious sacrifices made in Hiroshima and Nagasaki. *There must be no new Hibakusha!*

IPPNW's message has been carried from Nagasaki to Hiroshima during the past two weeks by 40 cyclists from 20 countries, who braved the heat and humidity of the Japanese summer to remind us all about the catastrophic effects of nuclear weapons and to advocate their abolition. The medical students who organized this tour – and previous bike tours in other parts of the world – are the future of our federation. Their energy, creativity, and determination inspire all of us and give us the confidence to believe that there will never be another Hiroshima, that there will never be another Nagasaki, and that the coming generations will inherit a more peaceful world.

* * *

NON-ALIGNED MOVEMENT MEETING IN IRAN
NUCLEAR DISARMAMENT, NOT PROLIFERATION!

The Japan Council against A and H Bombs (Gensuikyo) sent the following message to the 16th Summit of Heads of State or Government of the Non-Aligned Movement, meeting in Tehran, Iran from 26 to 31 August 2012. Hiroshi TAKA, representative director of Gensuikyo, presented the message in person.

On the occasion of the 16th summit of Heads of State or Government of the Non-Aligned Movement, we extend warmest greetings of solidarity to you, and through you to the people each of you represent, from the movement against atomic and hydrogen bombs working in Japan, the only A-bombed country in the world.

During the period of the Cold War, which followed the end of World War Two, the Non-aligned Movement played the key role in establishing a peaceful and just world order based on the UN Charter, by opposing the division of the world by military blocs and the nuclear arms race, and firmly promoting non-alignment, national independence and sovereignty, the resolution of international conflicts be peaceful means and the establishing of a new international economic order. Further, the Non-aligned Movement kept warning of the danger of another Hiroshima or Nagasaki, and took the lead in international politics to totally ban nuclear weapons. With the passing of some 20 years since the end of the Cold War, we firmly believe that the role of the Non-Aligned Movement is now more important than ever before in achieving these objectives.

Our movement developed in 1954, in protest against the massive damage and contamination caused by the hydrogen bomb test conducted by the United States of America at Bikini Atoll in the Pacific Ocean on 1

March that year. Since then, we have developed grassroots actions and international solidarity to achieve three basic objectives of 1) the prevention of nuclear war, 2) a total ban and the elimination of nuclear weapons, and 3) relief and solidarity with the *Hibakusha*, the A-bomb sufferers, including the World Conference against A and H Bombs held in Hiroshima and Nagasaki every summer, nationwide signature campaigns in support of the start of negotiations for a Nuclear Weapons Convention, and annual peace marches through all Japanese municipalities to raise public awareness for the abolition of nuclear weapons. Since the very start of our movement, we have always supported the principles and policies set out by the forerunners of the Non-Aligned Movement.

The 16th Non-Aligned Movement Summit meets at an extremely important juncture. The 8th Nuclear Non-Proliferation Treaty Review Conference, in May 2010, agreed that it would 'achieve the peace and security of a world without nuclear weapons' as principle and objective, and confirmed the 'unequivocal undertaking' of the Nuclear Five agreed in May 2000 to 'accomplish the total elimination of their nuclear arsenals'. It further affirmed that 'all States need to aim special efforts to establish the necessary framework to achieve and maintain a world without nuclear weapons', and specifically noted 'the Five-Point Proposal' of UN Secretary General Ban Ki-moon, which includes *inter alia* the 'negotiation of a nuclear weaponos convention'.

The final document also made it an obligation to convene an international conference for a Middle East Zone free of nuclear weapons as well as other weapons of mass destruction.

These agreements are not something that can be done when the Nuclear Five like. As Ambassador Libran Cabactulan, the chair of the 8th NPT Review Conference pointed out in his speech to the Preparatory Committee to the 2015 NPT Review Conference, in May this year, fortunately, the world has avoided a nuclear holocaust for some 60 years and, hopefully, for many years to come. But 'let us not continue to tempt the fates … The only way to ensure the prevention of a nuclear holocaust is to take away the nuclear option from the hands of men who are so fallible'.

We refuse all kinds of arguments intended to try to justify the continued possession of nuclear weapons, or modernization and new development of such weapons, or nuclear proliferation, such as 'nuclear deterrence' doctrine or 'nuclear umbrella' arguments. The goals agreed upon at the 2010 NPT Review Conference have to be, honestly and in good faith, translated into action towards the next, 2015 NPT Review Conference and, above all, the negotiations on the nuclear weapons convention must start without any further delay, to build a legally binding framework needed to create and maintain a nuclear weapons-free world.

On 2 to 9 August this year, the 2012 World Conference against A and H Bombs was held in Hiroshima and Nagasaki. We listened to the enlightening and prescient views of Ms Angela Kane, UN High Representative for Disarmament Affairs, government representatives of Egypt, Malaysia, Cuba, Mexico, Norway, and others that are committed to abolishing nuclear weapons without delay. Nine thousand participants, including overseas delegates from 20 countries, as well as Japanese grassroots activists, renewed their determination to redouble their efforts to strengthen public support for nuclear disarmament. The document adopted by the Conference placed focus on the need for implementation of the agreements of the 2010 NPT Review Conference and, further, paid special attention to the Statements of the 16 Governments, including Non-aligned Movement members, New Agenda Coalition members, and neutral countries, set out at the last NPT Preparatory Committee.

Hiroshima and Nagasaki teach humanity that the use of nuclear weapons is a crime against humanity. The action to eliminate nuclear weapons concerns everyone, governments and civil society alike, for which all citizens around the world are to be invited. We, as the movement working in a country where people suffered the 'hell on earth', will do our best to make known to people around the world the reality of the two cities and their citizens on those days and thereafter, thus organising people in all different forms, including the petition campaign. These campaigns will be firmly in solidarity with your action, carried out together with peace movements around the world, as well as the Hibakusha.

The nuclear crisis caused by the severe accident at the Fukushima Daiichi Power Plant continues. More than 160,000 people are still living in refuges. As the movement with the slogan 'No More Hibakusha', we are also working hard for the relief of those suffering, for an end to dependency on nuclear power plants, and for development and a switch to sustainable energy. In overcoming these problems facing humanity, achieving a total ban on nuclear weapons will open a new page. Of this there is no doubt.

Before concluding, we wish you every success in the work of the 16th Summit of the Non-Aligned Movement.

Reviews

Leila

Sarah Irving, *Leila Khaled: Icon of Palestinian Liberation*, Pluto Press, 2012, 168 pages, hardback ISBN 9780745329529, £45, paperback ISBN 9780745329512, £12.99

An account of Leila Khaled's dedicated and inspirational life is long overdue. Sarah Irving's book fills the gap admirably. It is based solidly on Khaled's own accounts of her life in interviews both with the author and others, as well as archival material, newspaper reports and the like.

Sarah Irving's biography of Leila Khaled is as much an account of the Palestinian struggle for freedom, as it is an account of Khaled's life. So it should be. Leila Khaled's life, from an infancy traumatized by the Nakba, through her youth as a refugee driven to militant opposition to theft of her homeland, to her later years in ongoing political activity, has been so closely woven into the Palestinian struggle against occupation and oppression, as to make the two inseparable.

It would be almost impossible to write a biography of Leila Khaled without mention of 'the defining hijackings of 1969 and 1970'. Those are, after all, what brought both Leila Khaled and – as Khaled and her comrades intended – the Palestinian struggle, to world attention. The hijackings did more than that. They also served as inspiration to those engaged in struggles for freedom elsewhere. Far away in the townships of South Africa, for example, Khaled and her comrades became icons of resistance for a generation of oppressed and exploited young people, most of whose own leaders were then murdered, imprisoned, banned and exiled by an apartheid state to which the Israeli state would in years to come be likened.

Irving's book moves swiftly over Khaled's 'iconic' status, notwithstanding the subtitle of the book. As Irving makes clear from the outset, Khaled has been much more than the 'beautiful girl hijacker'. Her life has encompassed the roles of 'wife and mother, teacher and campaigner, member of the Palestinian National Council and leader of the General Union of Palestinian Women'. It has been a life devoted almost exclusively to political and military struggle – both before and since the hijackings.

Khaled was just a little girl of four at the time of the Nakba – the Catastrophe – during which Zionist terrorists began what was to become an ongoing drive to force Palestinians from their homeland. With her family she fled her native Haifa for a refugee camp in Lebanon. Khaled was not to see Haifa again until she hijacked a plane to make the world aware of her people's sufferings. In the course of the hijacking, she made the pilot fly over Haifa.

Scarcely more than a decade after that forced politicization, fifteen-year-old Khaled became a member of the Arab Nationalist Movement, a branch of which later became the left-wing Popular Front for the Liberation of Palestine. Khaled trained as one of the PFLP's fighters and it was as such that she engaged in those historic hijackings. The course of Khaled's life as a student, as a daughter, as a wife, as a mother were from the outset determined by what was required of her politically – constantly on the move, constantly under threat, constantly, with those she loved, in danger. Nothing, however, could deter her from giving her all to the struggle of her people, not even the terrible loss of a sister to the terrorists seeking to take Leila Khaled's own life, or the pain of several bouts of plastic surgery which would enable her to continue her political activities in the face of those wishing to kill her.

Over the decades since the seventies, the nature of Khaled's contribution to the Palestinian struggle necessarily changed from a military one to a political one. From soldier and hijacker she moved into political activism in refugee camps and in the women's movement, a leadership role nationally, and becoming an international representative of, and spokesperson for, the movement against the ongoing occupation of Palestine. No longer armed with guns and grenades, she none the less remains a fierce fighter for real freedom for the Palestinian people, rejecting bogus accords and peace processes as well as dummy authorities which fall far short of what she believes in: freedom for the Palestinian people from occupation and oppression, return of their land, the right of all Palestinians to return to their homeland in peace. Just as she inspired those engaged in struggle elsewhere with her militant actions, she continues to do so by her ongoing expressions of support for struggles of oppressed people elsewhere in the world. A true internationalist, Khaled stands not just for social justice for Palestinians, but for social justice for all people.

Now in her sixties, with decades of struggle and many personal sacrifices behind her, Khaled has no intention of retiring from the fight for Palestinian rights. Her commitment to doing all she can to promote the cause of the Palestinian people is undimmed by age. As she says: 'You can't retire from struggle, or from being involved'. *Aluta continua!*

Filled as it is with the twists and turns of the Palestinian liberation movement, and all the organizations and personalities which have comprised it before and during Khaled's lifetime, Irving's book is pretty dense. But it remains an accessible chronicle of the life of a remarkable woman and the struggle which has been the focal point of that life. As such, it deserves to be read by everyone interested not only in the Palestinian struggle, but also in the struggle against oppression and exploitation everywhere.

My daughter has just returned from a stint as a volunteer in Palestine and is already engrossed in Irving's book. She wants to recommend it to all her fellow volunteers. I am sending a copy to Cape Town, to one of the many Leilas whose parents were amongst those influenced by Leila Khaled.

Shereen Pandit

Downwinders

Kristen Iversen, *Full Body Burden: Growing Up in the Shadow of a Secret Nuclear Facility*, Harvill Secker, London, 2012, 416 pages, paperback ISBN 9781846556142, £14.99

The drive south from the eclectic, activist prone, posh parts of Boulder follows the Rocky Mountains, one of the most impressive North American mountain ranges, into the huddled suburbs of Denver: Broomfield, Westminster, Arvada, Golden. In half an hour's drive, looking on the right, one can take in the theatrical peaks of Boulder Mountain Park and the pine covered red rocks of Eldorado Canyon, and on the left, the extended mass of metropolitan Denver, with the city's impressive skyline showcasing its 56-story Republic Plaza and the Qwest Tower. Just before entering the city, the Rocky Flats National Wildlife Refuge catches the eye; home to the threatened Preble's meadow jumping mouse, the refuge seems to fit perfectly in the idyllic setting of one of the most green and environmentally savvy states. Established in 2007, the refuge is yet to be open to the public, since controversy over its nuclear-weapons-plant past and evidence of plutonium and uranium traces in the soil would make anybody think twice before entering the site for a Sunday stroll.

Leaving no stone unturned of the Rocky Flats National Wildlife Refuge's contentious existence, Kristen Iversen brings forth *Full Body Burden*, a memoir of her family's imminent downfall, paralleled with the institutionalised web of lies surrounding Rocky Flats Plant, one of the United States' Cold War legacies.

The family universe is poetically reconstructed and evocative of the television series *Mad Men:* it is the 1960s, dad is a successful lawyer in the city; mum is a housewife, mother of three and over the moon about the move to the heavenly suburb of Bridledale; the children ride ponies, chase rabbits, have teenage identity crises and first romances. From the family's favourite pastimes, driving through the Colorado Rockies on a Sunday and grown-ups enjoying cocktails in the evening, the latter proves to be more dangerous and leads, within a decade, to the slow-paced, taciturn end of the family, the American dream and the post-war promises; the law practice, the big house, the ponies, the marriage, and the innocence of the children all vanish.

Meanwhile, two miles west, past the strikingly beautiful Standley Lake, the Rocky Flats Nuclear Weapons Plant is in full production, from 1952 to 1989, manufacturing more than seventy thousand plutonium triggers, the hearts of every nuclear weapon made in America. With a heightened investigative style, Iversen manages to cover in detail the tumultuous history of the plant, without transforming the novel into a stale Environmental Protection Agency report. The novelty in her approach is the seemingly effortless inclusion of former workers' and activists' experiences and stories; thus, the reader meets the design engineer Jim Stone, security guards Stan and Bill, lab workers Debbie and Jacque, activist Sisters Pat and Pam, rancher Marcus Church, Dr. Johnson and attorney Holme, FBI agent Jon Lipsky and many others.

With the help of almost two hundred accounts and interviews, and Iversen's further research, Rocky Flats is unmasked as 'the most dangerously contaminated site' in America, with unofficial reports claiming plutonium contamination of the soil and nitrate contamination of water supplies, radioactive rabbits and cattle, 2,600 pounds of plutonium unaccounted for, and a significantly higher rate of cancer of the lung, liver, bone and bone marrow and other life threatening illnesses for the nearby residents.

Full Body Burden also follows the development of Cook v. Rockwell International, an environmental class-action lawsuit seeking $500 million in damages for property owners whose house values have plummeted because of the Rocky Flats scandal; plaintiffs seeking financial compensation for health issues related to low-level radiation exposure encounter difficulties in providing a direct causal link between the pollution and the illnesses.

At the core of the book lies the parallel between the family memoir and the nuclear plant investigation, bridged by the leitmotifs of secrecy and voluntary ignorance. Here stands a rather difficult question to answer. Is this parallel successful or not? Throughout most of the eight chapters of the book, although these two universes intertwine chronologically, they don't seem to affect one another substantively. In other words, the parallel seems forced; the author herself admits that, for most of her childhood and life as a young adult, she was blissfully unaware of the dangers posed by Rocky Flats, even when she worked there as a temp. The juxtaposition of the two universes – both skilfully rendered and perfectly able to stand on their own – is constructed rather retrospectively, post the Rocky Flats era, as the author seems to savagely chase for meanings and connections. However, a series of intimate stories of friends and neighbours whose lives have been affected and, in some cases, terminated by diseases that can be traced back to radiation, find a place in the book and carry the difficult parallel through.

In terms of research, nobody can deny the exquisite result of a dozen years' work, and Iversen is particular about the transparency of her studies, at the back of the book recording, beyond Allen Ginsberg's 'Plutonian Ode' and Acknowledgements, thorough notes for individual chapters, a much needed timeline, and an Index.

After the Fukushima Nuclear Plant explosions, *Full Body Burden*, beyond being a captivating account of a 1960s American middle-class suburban family with all the tarnished hopes and gaffes of the Cold War era, becomes relevant to anybody who has ever doubted their government's pledge of working for the common good.

Lucia Sweet

Communists

Phil Piratin, *Our Flag Stays Red*, Lawrence & Wishart, 2006, 128 pages, paperback ISBN 9781905007288, 12.99

Although only glancing at it (p. 125 n. 42), the recently (2012) published biography of Bert Ramelson (born Baruch Rachmilevitch) by Roger Seifert and Tom Sibley provokes exhumation of this memoir of another once-famous communist of that time, Phil Piratin.

Originally published in 1948, this re-issue comes with an introductory well-annotated essay by John Callow taking Piratin's story down to his death in 1995, plus a smattering of cartoons and photographs, though regrettably without an index. It can be supplemented by the various newspaper obituaries (available online), most valuably that by Piratin's comrade, former *Daily Worker* editor, George Matthews (*Independent*, 18 December 1995).

To younger readers both Piratin and his beloved Communist Party of Great Britain are ancient history. A Jewish-born (1907) East Ender, Piratin grew up and remained in his native Stepney throughout the turbulent Thirties and the War years, the latter culminating in his 1945 election as Communist Member of Parliament for Mile End, winning 5,075 votes over Labour's 3,861 and Conservative's 1,722. At the 1950 Election, his constituency abolished, Piratin stood unsuccessfully in Stepney.

Along with the, by now, veteran Willie Gallacher, Piratin was the only other Communist in Westminster, summing up this dynamic duo's parliamentary tactics thus:

> 'I automatically moved and he seconded that he should be leader. He then appointed me as Chief Whip. Comrade Gallacher decides the policy and I make sure he carries it out.'

Major set-pieces in his memoir describe organising the East End's resistance to Mosley's fascists, culminating in the famous 'Battle of Cable Street' (4 October 1936) – all very different from the BBC's *EastEnders*; the struggle for tenants' rights and concomitant rent strikes; the celebrated invasion of the Savoy Hotel – a modern 'red top' headline would doubtless have read something like 'Savoy Grill-ed by Phil'; breaking into the underground, thereby forcing the government to abandon its criminal ban on using Tube stations as air-raid shelters.

Piratin recounts these exploits with verve, wit, and a seasoning of justifiable conceit. His anti-Mosley campaign was the inspiration, albeit more pessimistically reworked, for *Chicken Soup with Barley*, the first play in Arnold Wesker's celebrated trilogy. Wesker's own commitment to the working class was also manifest in his play *The Kitchen* and the founding (1964) of Centre 42 at the Roundhouse Theatre.

It is probably no coincidence that some of the momentous issues of the 1930s were reflected in ideologically unsympathetic literary quarters. P. G. Wodehouse's Roderick Spode memorably ridicules Mosley in *The Code of the Woosters*. Everard Webley in Aldous Huxley's *Point Counterpoint* looks (despite some critics' doubts) like his *Doppelganger*. Graham Greene's now largely forgotten and never filmed novel *It's a Battlefield* has (from a cynical viewpoint) communists and communism at its centre, also industrial unrest among women workers at a match factory – Greene himself summed up his dominant theme as 'the injustice of man's justice'. The arch-Tory Anthony Powell was moved to include Marxists (Stalinist and Trotskyist), Pacifists, and fighting for the Republican cause in Spain in his epic *A Dance to the Music of Time*.

Most relevant, however, and most deserving to be revived and read alongside Piratin is Edward Upward's autobiographical trilogy of novels, *The Spiral Ascent,* comprising *In The Thirties, The Rotten Elements,* and *No Home But The Struggle.* They tell the story of a poet and his wife joining the Party, first to combat Mosley, then after the War the alleged 'Revisionism' of the new leadership's increasing leaning to a parliamentary rather than revolutionary road to Socialism.

Apart from a passing compliment to Lenin's *The State and Revolution,* Piratin has little to say about this issue (in contrast with Ramelson), preferring to concentrate on the day-to-day struggles on his home patch and viewing his time at Westminster as fruitful. One imagines his conviction (justified in retrospect) that Stalin's Socialism in One Country made more immediate sense than Trotsky's notion of Permanent Revolution. Were Piratin alive today, he would be asking some very practical questions about Leon's dreamier disciples. How can the workers be armed? Without the CPGB, who will lead them into Revolution? One of the competing Trotskyist/ite groupuscules? If the latter, would their first concern be 'proceeding to construct the Socialist order' or liquidating their sectarian rivals?

According to Seibert and Sibley (p. 35), 'We have no record of Ramelson's personal reaction to the Hitler-Stalin pact'. Piratin largely glosses over it, with no mention of the agonising debates it caused among the Party's top brass, minutely documented by Francis King and George Matthews in *About Turn: The British Communist Party and the Second World War: The Verbatim Record of the Central Committee Meetings of 25 September and 2-3 October 1939* (Lawrence & Wishart, 1990; cf. Peter Fryer's detailed review in the *Encyclopedia of Trotskyism On-Line).* For Piratin and company, the trouble was that their standard defence that Stalin was sensibly buying time had to ignore the simple fact that he needed this hiatus because his massive purges of the officer corps had left the Red Army unfit to fight.

Nowadays, beyond the *Morning Star* and memories of veteran members/ex-members, the CPGB is generally consigned to Trotsky's 'Dustbin of History'. Some year ago, Ken Coates (who broke with it over Tito) mentioned to me in a letter that he nevertheless thought the allegedly 'malign' role of the Party 'somewhat exaggerated'. Both those who hope he is right and those who hope he is wrong should go back to Piratin for his record (above reservations notwithstanding) of the Party at its best. *Our Flag Stays Red* deserves to stay read.

Barry Baldwin

The Religion of Art

Fiona MacCarthy, *The Last Pre-Raphaelite: Edward Burne-Jones and the Victorian Imagination*, Faber and Faber, 656 pages, hardback ISBN 978-0571228614, £25, paperback ISBN 9780571228621, £17.99

This is the latest of Fiona MacCarthy's biographies, following upon William Morris, Byron and Eric Gill, and it is certainly the most deeply researched and heaviest – 656 pages, including sixty pages of references and a forty page Index. My hands and arms ached from holding it, but it was well worth the effort. I have called this review 'The Religion of Art' because Burne-Jones himself said that he gave up the Christian religion in which he was reared for what he called 'the Religion of Art'.

MacCarthy makes it quite clear that this was not just 'art for art's sake'. There was a serious purpose behind Burne-Jones's art. In a telling phrase, MacCarthy quotes him saying that 'he negates the possibility of human littleness'. He called on his pupils to 'look for beauty', and in MacCarthy's words, 'his philosophy of art' lies in 'his conviction that a life lived through beauty was every body's birthright, regardless of their income and social position'.

MacCarthy makes a special point of Burne-Jones's painting of *King Cophetua and the Beggar Maid*, that was greeted with acclaim in 1884, that it 'encapsulated many bitter conflicts of the Victorian age and it established Burne-Jones on a new footing as the most important painter of his time'. 'It is the stark contrasts,' she writes, 'between capitalists and under-classes, between the factory owners and the workers' that informs his art.

It is a serious problem for any reader that while some of the portraits are reproduced in colour, larger pieces like *King Cophetua and the Beggar Maid* are much reduced and in the black and white of the photogravure. Fortunately, in late 2012, it is possible to go to the Tate Gallery, to see a major collection of Pre-Raphaelite paintings and drawings, and I strongly recommend a visit.

There could be no book about Burne-Jones that was not also about William Morris, with whom – with just one breakdown over political differences towards the end of Morris's life – Burne-Jones collaborated in brotherly artistic and business endeavours. It was Burne-Jones, MacCarthy reminds us, who invented the term 'Arts and Crafts' for the exhibition that covered Morris & Co.'s designs for tapestries, embroideries, wallpapers, curtains, painted furniture, stained glass, that came from the pens and brushes of Burne-Jones and Morris. It was, moreover, at the Working Men's College that Burne-Jones studied under Madox Brown.

The political rift between Burne-Jones and Morris, after 1883, when Morris joined Hyndman's Marxist Democratic Federation and, later, formed the even more revolutionary Socialist League, is a sad story told very sympathetically by MacCarthy. Burne-Jones had liked Ruskin's *Fors Clavigera* and *Unto this Last* (which my father gave me to read when I was 16, and confirmed me as a life-long socialist), and Burne-Jones had opposed his nephew, Rudyard Kipling's, imperialist defence of the South African War. Ruskin could attack the capitalist system but, for Burne-Jones, Morris was an artist and a poet, and should stick to his last. The rift with Morris was healed before Morris died

MacCarthy reveals Burne-Jones showing awareness that he was mixing with an aristocratic and wealthy set, but his closest friends in the aristocracy, the painter George Howard 9th Earl of Carlisle and his wife Rosalind, had left-wing views. Burne-Jones's wife, Georgiana, was pro-Boer in the South African War, and continued to take Morris's *The Commonweal*, after Burne-Jones rejected it. She was a suffragette and, after Burne-Jones's death, became a socialist and member of the Labour Party and local councillor.

MacCarthy deals with Burne-Jone's relationship with Georgiana with extreme delicacy and empathy. The great love of Burne-Jones's life was, unquestionably, his model, the Greek Maria Zambaco, whom Georgiana somehow tolerated. But Burne-Jones had a succession of beautiful young girls for whom he developed an overpowering passion, leaving him distraught when they became engaged to be married. Several of them are shown in MacCarthy's book reproduced in colour, and reveal how, in Burne-Jones's words, the artist 'reaches into that inner soul, the psyche of the subject'. Burne-Jones's love for his own children is beyond doubt – Phil and Margaret – Margaret who married Mackail, founder of Morris & Co., and author of Morris's biography.

This book of Fiona MacCarthy's is so full of fascinating references to famous people that a few have to be mentioned in a review. First perhaps Gladstone, about whose death Burne-Jones is quoted as saying, 'So that great creature is gone'. Burne-Jones designed a memorial glass window for the Gladstone family at Hawarden. Then, at the other end of the Party spectrum, stood Stanley Baldwin, son of Burne-Jones's cousin, Alfred, who shared with his father and Burne-Jones's son, Philip, the watches over the coffin, before the cremation at Burne-Jones's death. Another close relative of Burne-Jones was Rudyard Kipling, his favourite nephew, for whom Burne-Jones is shown as having mixed feelings. MacCarthy quotes him at first responding enthusiastically to Kipling's famous *Recessional*, but then having second thoughts about the battle cry of jingo-politics. Henry James is quoted by MacCarthy as meeting with Burne-Jones 'a couple of times at the thrilling, throbbing Parnell trial'. For Burne-Jones, MacCarthy writes, 'the arraignment of Parnell was an agonising demonstration of English hypocrisy', and she adds, 'bringing about his final disenchantment with political and public life'.

There are interesting references to the Left political interest in Burne-Jones – an exhibition of the *Briar Rose* paintings at Toynbee Hall. These paintings were purchased by Alexander Henderson, later Lord Faringdon, who married the widow of the editor of *The Daily Worker*. But, as an Africanist, I like best the fact that in the tapestry of *The Star of Bethlehem* at Merton Abbey, one of the Magi, as the King of Nubia, is black.

To end this review, Fiona MacCarthy has given me the perfect envoi in the words she quotes from the gardener at Kipling's house, where the grave rests:

> 'What did strike me about him,' Marten said, 'was his humanity. There aint too many humane men in the world today.'

You can say that again!

Michael Barratt Brown

Human Touch

Alex Strick van Linschoten and Felix Kuehn, *Poetry of the Taliban*, Hurst & Company 2012, 224 pages, hardback ISBN 9781849041119, £14.99

Islamist militants, suicide bombers, *hadjis* or terrorists, the Taliban have been given multiple names and identities, mainly by the Western media. Since 9/11 they have lived on the battlefield and they have fought on the *wrong* side; they instantly became the enemies, of freedom, of religious tolerance, of the 21st century.

Through the vastly publicised *Poetry of the Taliban*, Van Linschoten and Kuehn, Kandahar-based veterans of Afghan recent history, are seeking to expose a Taliban world beyond what is common knowledge, offer a human touch to a much derided populace, append poems and Pashto literature to guns and a survivalist culture. An audacious attempt by editors and publishers alike, the book was dubbed 'enemy propaganda' by a former commander of British forces in Afghanistan, and has attracted controversy, anonymous threats, as well as literary praise. With that said, *Poetry of the Taliban* has an in-built pick-up-and-see-for-yourself factor!

Presenting 235 carefully selected poems, also approved by and uploaded on the Taliban website, the anthology includes love poems, pastoral verses and patriotic ballads, and illustrates universally familiar leitmotivs such as heartbreak, sacrifice, doubt, courage and hatred.

One of the attributes of this project is the exploration of a much overlooked literature. With Afghanistan historically being at the centre of many trade and migration routes, it benefited from a rich blend of cultures and still exhibits diverse people and ethnicities: the Pashtuns, Tajiks, Hazaras, Uzbeks, Turkmen, Baloch and others. From a literary standpoint, it is appealing to take a closer look at the traditional *Tarana* oral ballads, translated from Pashto and depicting fighting and dying, such as these verses from *Pamir*, by Faizani:

> *I know the black, black mountains;*
> *I know the desert and its problems.*
> *My home is the mountain, my village is the mountain and I live in the*
> *   mountains;*
> *I know the black ditches.*
> *...*
> *I am the eagle of Spin Ghar's high peaks;*
> *I know Pamir's canyons.*
> *I walk through it day and night;*
> *I know the bends of Tor Ghar.*

Another characteristic form of verse is the beautiful *ghazal*, with rhyming couplets and a refrain, arguably Shakespearian in musicality and rhythm, although often without continuity of narrative, which is its most original and commendable feature. The *ghazal* has a rich history, having originated in sixth century Arabia and flourishing with the writings of the thirteenth and fourteenth century Persian poets, Rumi and Hafiz. It became a mark of Urdu and Pashto literature in the seventeenth century, Rahman Baba being a prominent poet of the movement that deals with melancholy, love, longing, and metaphysical questions. The German poet and philosopher Goethe experimented with the form, as did the Spanish poet Federico Garcia Lorca.

A good example of a *ghazal* in its original form is Khairkhwa's poem titled 'Injured', in the anthology's Human Cost section:

> *I stoned him with the stones of light tears*
> *Then I hung my sorrow on the gallows like Mansour.*
> *Like those who have been killed by the infidels,*
> *I counted my heart as one of the martyrs.*
> *It might have been the wine of our memory*
> *That made my heart drunk five times.*
> *The more I kept the secret of my love,*
> *This simple* ghazal *spoke more of my secrets.*
> *The one who gave you his trust,*
> *That person neglected you.*
> *I was injured, my brother was martyred,*
> *My stepmother watched me.*
> *O poem of Khairkhwa! I will accept your perfection*
> *If you guide back one of those who have fallen astray.*

Notice the seemingly autonomous couplets, with references to nationalistic spirit and heroes of the fatherland, romantic love, hardships of friendship, despair and loss. Commonly, the *ghazal* also includes the name of the poet in the last couplet, a technique called *takhallus*. The mentioning of 'wine' and 'drunk' is done symbolically, without appealing to the profane meanings of the words; this is particular to Afghan aesthetics and, although the imagery used is ordinary (with words such as 'gallows', 'nightingale', 'flower' often present), the interpretation brings forth a different dimension for every read – or recitation – of the same poem.

Although the editors have divided the entries into six different categories, one could argue that there is one theme visible all throughout: the war. References to the invaders, the 'infidels', the 'cruel oppressors' suggest that the war has forever altered and contaminated every sliver of Afghan life:

> *You come out of the nice city of lights.*
> *You are seeking your life in our black walls.*
> *
>
> *O son of our tribes! Don't sell yourselves to the Americans.*
> *
>
> *The army of the crazed crusaders will withdraw*
> *If our zealous* ghazis *fight.*
> *

The house of my history and culture was looted today,
Each slave is now riding me;
The teeth of the East and West have become like pliers on my muscles.
...
Who made a night raid on my house again?

The unforeseen and welcome theme is that of love, be it for a woman or a comrade of arms. It is the section that most closely accomplishes the editors' semi-secret wish, which is to portray the Taliban in a new, softer light.

Separation from you dried my eyes,
You were not blessed in the holy bosom.
In this sad journey of looking for you,
I haven't remembered you in every place.
*

Your love aside, what else is there?
It is like approaching the desert.
Like the dust on your footsteps.

Politically, this anthology is bound to be divisive. Literarily, it stands miles apart from contemporary perception of aesthetics, but it is an endless and fairly uncharted source of middle-eastern folklore, which is enough of a selling point for any literary critic and/or connoisseur who hasn't yet dabbled in the legends of Mansour and Malalai. Finally, the book's covert mission was to explore a different side of one of the twenty-first century's most puzzling characters; propagandistic or not, the anthology does indeed infuse personality and moral fibre into what were formally mere sketches of the Afghan Taliban.

Lucia Sweet

Moves

Guy Arnold, *Migration: Changing the World*, Pluto Press, London, 2011, 282 pages, hardback ISBN 9780745329062, £60, paperback ISBN 9780745329055, £ 19.99

Migration, of course, is a part of life and so, naturally, has been with us since the beginning of time: plants, birds, animals all do it and always have done so, human beings, too. The author concentrates on the last 60 years of the phenomenon.

The mass of statistics about the movement of millions of people can become a bit overwhelming, but you can hardly expect anything else in a book on migration. You can plough through it (it's worth it), do some judicious skipping, and read about the countries that interest you most, or do it the easy way and just read the *Introduction* and *Tentative Conclusions*. They, together, make a first class essay, but you would miss wee gems like the one statistic that fascinated me:

> 'In the early years of the Napoleonic wars, up to a third of the sailors on Nelson's fleet were blacks Shanghaied from the (Caribbean) islands.'

In his introduction, Guy Arnold makes a lot of projections about the masses of people on the planet by 2050 and quotes UN forecasts. He quotes Prof. Aubrey Manning of Edinburgh University who is horrified at the idea of so many more people on the planet and, come to that, so many more people in Britain. Neither the Earth nor the country can sustain such hordes. The author snaps back, 'The debate was less concerned with sustainability than with arguing against further immigration'. In his mouth, this is something of a sneer: he does *not* like people who are anti-immigration, and with good reason; racism is never far away. The way the UK treats its immigrants makes up some of the darkest pages in *Migration*. However, the author quotes James Lovelock, 'The Environmentalist' (of Gaia fame) who comes to the rescue and seems to contradict the UN's look into the future, when 'pestilence, war and famine will have dealt with the majority of humans'.

Arnold is very good on economic migrants. He insists that they have not come to scrounge off the welfare state. On the contrary, they have come to *work*. They are usually young, usually men, except those from the Philippines (your Filipino maid?), and are full of energy and initiative. The layabouts stay at home and lay about. The migrants run appalling risks on their journeys, drowning in their thousands in overcrowded, leaky boats or dying of thirst in their hundreds as they cross deserts. They are exploited and sometimes killed by ruthless people-trafficking gangs. In 2011, 80 were mowed down in one go. Others are thrown overboard.

> 'By mid 2007 there was a consensus that at least 6,000 Africans had perished attempting to cross the Mediterranean (the figure was based upon the number of bodies found, but many more would also have drowned without trace). The ruthlessness of traffickers is balanced by the desperation of the migrants, who entrust such people with their lives.'

Obviously, they are not in it for an easy ride. When and if they reach their destination, they are often treated abominably and work under appalling conditions:

> 'All they want is a chance to work. They don't mind putting in 12 hours a day or working on Saturdays and Sundays. They don't mind being paid a pittance, doing menial jobs and never getting a holiday. They will put up with bad working conditions that you or I would never tolerate. People fear they bring disease, but it's only the young and the very strong that can make this journey. All they want is to stay. Why are we so against them?'

Parts of the press hysterically denounce foreigners, sponging off the state and taking jobs away from the locals, in spite of the fact that migrants often do jobs that no one else wants. If there is no work for them, they tend to go back home or move on to another country where there is.

Big business rather likes them when there is no recession, because they *need* them, can pay them less, and don't have to worry so much about 'workers' rights'. The fascists hate them because they contaminate 'purity', spoil the 'British way of life', the 'American way of life', or the 'French way of life', whatever that means.

If a migrant survives all this, he or she can make what is considered good money. They send lots of it back home. For many countries, remittances are their biggest income, more than from traditional exports. They like their citizens to emigrate: they bring in good money and relieve unemployment and social unrest. The downside is that not only the poor, semi- and unskilled leave, but also the brightest and best, the brain drain. Scarce resources are spent on training them, only to be recruited by rich countries which take who they want and discard who they don't like.

The author also discusses internal migration: from the countryside to the city. For the first time in history, more people live an urban life rather than a rural one, which causes huge social upheaval; witness the rise of shantytowns, *favelas*, *villa miseries*, and *barrios marginados* around the world. The Chinese internal migration (as opposed to the very large diaspora) over recent years, including millions, is the greatest in history.

In his final section, *Tentative Conclusions,* Arnold writes:

> 'Over the years 1990-2010 a huge movement of people occurred worldwide. Some were refugees, asylum seekers or internally displaced people fleeing wars or other disasters, but the majority were economic migrants seeking a better life in countries other than their own.'

It can be hard to distinguish between refugees and economic migrants. Sometimes, it seems that more Salvadorans live in the United States than in El Salvador. No doubt, an exaggeration, but thousands left the country looking for a better life and thousands more fled a long and very nasty civil war. This is where I have reservations about the author's views. Sometimes migrants do predominate:

> 'Prior to the credit crunch, Dubai and the rest of the United Arab Emirates were estimated to have a population of 6.4 million of whom 5.5 million were foreigners.'

Although needed in such places for the élite's grandiose ideas of development, they are often treated disgracefully. At times, the host country might justifiably feel overwhelmed. Two million Iraqis fled their country after the American led invasion in 2003, with 9,000 people seeking asylum in the UK, 800 in the US, 18,000 in Sweden, and 6,000 in Australia. Jordan received 750,000 refugees, mostly unskilled, and Syria about a million. Up to October 2007, Syria maintained an open-door policy towards Iraqi refugees, but then began to feel the strain and see the impact on the locals, more concerned with the decreasing resources than with racial prejudice.

Take another example: under Mugabe, a quarter of Zimbabweans have left the country, with a large percentage ending up in nearby South Africa, adding to the country's high unemployment and, thus, not welcomed. It is probably true that all racists are anti-immigration, but it does not necessarily follow that all opposition to immigration is racist.

Arnold approves of Spain and Italy's humane decision that, 'when faced with large numbers of illegal immigrants, they solved the logistics of dealing with them by offering an amnesty', which meant that the migrants were free to travel north in search of work.

In the chaos that immigration sometimes is, several solutions emerge. One is to make the poor countries less poor, encouraging people to stay. Spain's former Prime Minister, Zapatero, said that the matter is of concern for all Europeans:

> 'We must work rapidly to reduce the gap in prosperity between Spain and Morocco and countries to the south of Morocco. The prosperity gap between Spain and Morocco is the largest in the world between bordering countries.'

The truth is that development, as usual, has been, more often than not, more to the advantage of the developers than those about to be developed, with the former exploiting, robbing, raping and despoiling the Third World for centuries. Now we are reaping the whirlwind harvest that was sown.

A second approach would be to build a wall like the Great Wall of China,

Hadrian's Wall, and Offa's Dyke, and the infamous Berlin Wall. These days there are also electrified wire fences; the Israelis, Americans, Indians and Saudis are building one each. Arnold says that, in the end, a wall or fence will make no difference; migrants will find a way (admittedly, more difficult and dangerous), whether it is through, over, under or round it.

One quibble, and I think it is a quibble, is that the word 'love' occurs only once in the whole book. Fair enough, it is about economic migrants and those fleeing death and destruction; yet separation of families, husbands and wives, parents and children, over long distances and long periods of time, has a devastating impact on heart and soul. Perhaps that is the subject of another book. As for this one, as I say, I flagged at times, but I kept at it. It was worth it. I learned a lot.

Nigel Potter

Down the Pit

Tom Hickman, *Called Up, Sent Down – The Bevin Boys' War*, History Press, 2010, 252 pages, paperback ISBN 9780752457499, £9.99

To keep the war machine running, Britain, during the Second World War, needed more and more coal. There wasn't enough so more miners were needed. Many miners had joined up, and they were not easily enticed to go back down the pit. The army was a cushier number! In desperation, Ernest Bevin decided to call up boys to work down the mines rather than join the forces. Most of these young men were disgusted. They wanted to fight for King and country, not work down the bloody pit. Of course, they had no choice, and this is their story.

It's not exactly D-Day or the Battle of the Bulge. I would not have bothered with it except my second father-in-law was, apparently, a 'Bevin Boy'. I was vaguely interested. (My first father-in-law taught maths to young pilots-to-be, who usually didn't return.) I bought a remaindered copy, and before sending it on to my stepdaughter I read it first, more out of a sense of duty. It turned out to be fascinating.

Bevin was serious about this conscription. He built hostels for the young called-up miners. It was not enough. Many had to live in digs, which varied from good to total squalor. The regular miners were kind enough to them once they had proved their worth. The regular miners themselves didn't care much about the war and were not especially patriotic. They would go on strike, war or no war, if they felt they were getting a raw deal.

Their main interests included beer and football, and when you have read this book you can see why. When you have worked a shift you are not much good for anything else: the sheer bloody hard physical labour. I felt exhausted just reading about it. Conditions were terrible, a bit like the trenches underground, admittedly without the shelling, but dangerous enough ('When you have to "go", lad, do it on tha shovel.')

If I had any choice (but, of course, one never does) I think I would take my chances storming up the beaches of Normandy rather than work down a mine. These 'Bevin Boys' and their miner mentors are some of the unsung heroes of World War Two.

Nigel Potter

Public Service

Jenny Manson (editor), *Public Services on the Brink,* Imprint Academic, 250 pages, paperback ISBN 9781845403065, £17.95

My interest in this collection is due to the fact that it's about how I derive my living; working in the public sector. Generally speaking, I have some concerns with compilations because they often include opinions (or, in the case of music, sounds) that offer no access point. This is the first compilation where I have not experienced such difficulties. With some books, the reader is confounded by obfuscation to the point that he or she puts the volume down. So it was with some satisfaction that, on reading this collection, I found that it was free of acronyms and unfathomable technical commentary. In fact, the contributions are written in a direct and clear manner. Personal experiences run through them in a way that helps the reader's engagement with what are generally very tough subjects. Often, when you talk to people, they will have a clear reason for using the particular public service they require; for example, 'Anna' in the piece on Legal Aid. But, I wonder, would she have a cogent appraisal of the overall requirement for public services?

Do I? I know that I want public services for myself at those times when a simple piece of practical, professional insight can save hours of wasted and misdirected effort. But I also want such services to assist those in the society around me in the moments when they experience desperate need and distress. Sadly, 'Anna's' difficult case is a regular and almost common experience for too many of our citizens. Other such experiences of public service go even deeper and may be even more complicated and upsetting.

Each experience needs careful consideration, a degree of empathy beyond the usual boundaries, and insights that can usually only be gained from access at a professional level.

Nor is it solely a question of the legalities surrounding personal distress. For example, in the section on the NHS there is an exposé of the 'Paperless Mountain', which brought a smile to my lips. The opening line of this section reads: 'a key aspect of good care is record keeping', which is not rocket science, but the author then spells out another difficult truth that confronts those of us working in the public services. This is about '... the triumph of form over substance and an assumption that people doing the job cannot be relied upon'.

At this point, I knew that this was why public services were indeed perceived as being 'on the brink', with the media shoving them over the edge. There are 'managers' and 'bureaucrats' currently in public service, depicted honestly here, who have been converted to the cause of 'self interest'. They may well have been committed to public service in the remote recesses of their memories, but they are now being bought off all too easily and rapidly.

The underlying theme of each of these pieces is that we are suddenly being told at every turn, and at every opportunity, that public service should pay for itself. It should be managed just like any household budget. This theme began with a comment made by Margaret Thatcher, and it has grown into the latest fashionable tool to promote a neoliberal agenda. The proposal is that every action and every process in the public service should show a profit, be disposed of, or changed into a profitable adaptation of such a service.

Were such assertions true, there would be no need for the word 'service' at all; it could easily be replaced by the word 'business'. But true public service cannot be replaced by business, despite governments telling the public sector that private industry will successfully take over its functions. This has proved a disaster at every turn. The private sector, one contribution asserts, is very good at micro management, but it is incapable of the macro management required by government. The security débâcles at the London Olympics and the Royal Jubilee have exposed that myth. The private sector is good at exploitative conduct and extracting the maximum money for itself regardless of performance. It seduces managers with the size of the potential salaries and bonuses they can achieve despite, or regardless of, performance. Such individuals are the means by which some politicians seek to return society to a time when their forebears were in absolute control.

The final chapter of *Public Services on the Brink* gives some insight into such a scheme. I have myself witnessed the witch-hunts of trade unionists whose opinions do not conform to those advocating a neoliberal cash grab. The fundamental and cogent arguments advanced by such trade unionists cannot easily be refuted, even by long serving hacks in the media. This chapter quite rightly asserts that the tactic is, if you cannot beat the argument, then smear and vilify the person, whether they are trade union leaders with substantial profiles, or middle-ranking activists subject to blacklisting because they have raised health and safety concerns. In some instances, trade unionists have had their entire working lives blighted because they have shown concern for their colleagues.

This is a very good book, well written and tightly edited. But, more importantly, it provides many of the essential insights and arguments that clearly explain why public service is essential to all of us. You cannot easily dispose of the profiteering pariahs, as seen in the section on the railways, but many have successfully mitigated and countered the disjointed and false neoliberal arguments for profit from public services. If you did not have a coherent picture of public service provision before reading *Public Services on the Brink*, it should assist considerably in providing arguments to support institutions that are an essential ingredient in our society, and are pivotal to us becoming the people we aspire to be.

Dave Putson

Alliances No More

Panagiotis Dimitrakis, *Failed Alliances of the Cold War: Britain's Strategy and Ambitions in Asia and the Middle East*, I.B. Tauris, 2012, 256 pages, hardback ISBN 9781848859746, £52.50

In a carefully resourced work, Panagiotis Dimitrakis examines the history of the creation, existence and demise of the Central Treaty Organization (CENTO) and the South-East Asia Treaty Organization (SEATO). Drawing upon primary research of the latest declassified British and American intelligence assessments, diplomatic dispatches and military plans, he has written a compelling and important new work of Cold War history[1].

Dimitrakis divides his book into seven chapters: 'Britain and the United States: Shaping alliances beyond NATO'; 'Pakistan's strategy'; 'CENTO's Nuclear Bombers and Cyprus'; 'SEATO: Planning and Divisions'; 'SEATO and Vietnam'; 'The Shah and CENTO'; and 'Demise of the

Alliances'. Together with the brief Introduction and the Conclusion the main text is 186 pages, followed by 34 pages of notes – mostly to recently declassified material – and eight pages of bibliography.

As the author states in his introduction:

> 'The central argument of this book, assessing British and, to a lesser extent, American strategy and ambitions for CENTO and SEATO, is that the absence of a Russian and/or Chinese threat of invasion led to the demise of these alliances, since key regional members – notably Iran and Pakistan – lost their interest in continuing with the organizations. No actual deterrence was ever implemented, because there was no real threat to be deterred in the first place. Besides, all the allies showed themselves willing to make only qualified commitments to the defence plans. The Indo-Pakistani wars, the Vietnam war, the détente with Soviet Russia and finally the fall of the Shah of Iran in 1979 cost SEATO and CENTO their very existence.'

In the first chapter, Dimitrakis examines the attitude prevalent in the US towards the creation of anti-communist alliances in Asia and the Middle East during and after the Korean war in order to contain the USSR, and compares it with the UK motives towards alliance-building:

> 'On the British side, the key motivations for building alliances had been two: first, Britain needed to preserve her world-power status in Europe, Asia and the Middle East ... The second motivation was that Britain needed a great deal of help in this endeavour ...'

On the same page, however, it is pointed out that there was a third incentive, reminiscent of situations vividly depicted in *Dr. Stangelove*:

> 'Indeed the Foreign Office feared that unless Washington was not bound by some sort of formal alliance in Asia and the Middle East, they would "drag, by unilateral action, the western world into a full scale war with China – or worse".'[2]

In addition to comparisons of the US versus UK motivations towards alliance building, and comparisons (and differentiations) between the NATO and CENTO/SEATO treaties, the first chapter also includes reference to other alliances in the Pacific area; the Australia, New Zealand, United States Security Treaty (ANZUS), the US-Japan Mutual Security Treaty, the non-military Colombo Plan for economic and social development, and so on. Incidentally, in the case of the latter there arises an interesting example of the value and continuing endurance of a *non-military* pact:

> 'Britain's stance towards the SEATO was ambivalent – in the light of strong pressure from the Treasury not to expand overseas commitments. Already the "Colombo Plan" had shown that a non-military pact of mutual economic and

technical aid could be successful with non-aligned nations. It was signed in January 1950 by Britain, Australia, New Zealand, Ceylon, Pakistan and India, with Laos acceding in 1951. A year later Burma, Thailand, Nepal, and the Philippines joined, followed by Indonesia in 1953. Other states acceding were Japan (1954), Bhutan and South Korea (1962), Maldives and Afghanistan (1963), Iran and Singapore (1966), Bangladesh and Fiji (1972), New Guinea (1973), and Vietnam and Mongolia (2004). The United States had signed in February 1951, on the understanding that the Colombo Plan was no more than "informal and advisory"[3]. The Plan drew upon British resources and increased spending on aid packages; but most significantly the pact demonstrated that it could survive Cold War antagonisms as well as regional members' suspicions of each other.'

This example of non-military co-operation exhibiting such resilience over time contrasts perfectly with the content of the second chapter, dealing with the main Pakistani motive for participation in CENTO and SEATO, i.e. their envisioned value in Indo-Pakistani antagonism. Dimitrakis examines in detail the Pakistani aspirations as a *paradigm* of the complications and disappointments (for all parties involved) likely to arise from persistent effort of an alliance member to exploit its membership to gain military strength (and free armaments) against an antagonist *not included* – neither in letter nor in spirit – in the list of threats of the alliance.

Another such paradigm, on a grander scale, is examined in detail in chapters four and five, which are probably the most interesting parts of the book for the general reader. Those chapters examine the original rationale for the creation of SEATO (chapter four) and then the frustrated American aspirations regarding the use of SEATO's forces against North Vietnam, a country not designated as 'a threat' by the Manila Treaty. Chapter five also examines the Labour Government's (under Harold Wilson) refusal to acquiesce to any endeavour which could potentially lead to UK entanglement in the Vietnam war.

In the third chapter Dimitrakis devotes 14 pages to the strategic British 'sovereign' bases in Cyprus which hosted an RAF nuclear 'deterrent' force as a permanent supporting element of CENTO's military plans. It is worth noting that this force (composed of two British Canberra nuclear bomber squadrons and, later, a Vulcan squadron) was the sole element of UK (or US) combat forces committed exclusively to CENTO. This force, plus valuable intelligence-gathering installations, was based in Cyprus at the time of the country's struggle for national independence and later, during the sixties, of strife between the Greek-Cypriot and Turkish-Cypriot communities. This chapter is thus of value for historians endeavouring to access the various complicated politico-military parameters exerting heavy influence on the island's recent tortured history.

The sixth chapter focuses on the late Shah, while bringing to light a trove of diplomatic and intelligence assessments about the situation in Iran, the possibility of a threat via Afghanistan, and so on. It gives a vivid portrait of an autocrat whose grandiose and, at the same time, idiosyncratic and insecure character contributed to the unravelling of CENTO; the alliance was recognized as a relic by all participants already in the mid-seventies, the era of *détente*. But its death knell was sounded when Iran withdrew from the alliance soon after the Islamic revolution. It is a useful chapter, in lieu of the current international focus on Iran.

On the whole, *Failed Alliances* could be a very attractive and illuminating book for the historically inclined general reader, thanks to the good organization of the material and the author's astute observations. On the other hand, the very careful and extensive documentation, based on recently declassified material, makes *Failed Alliances* a 'must read' for the specialists – particularly historians and active diplomats – and a useful source for international relations students.

Theodore N. Iliadis

Notes

1 The two alliances were created in the fifties in order to deter the perceived Soviet threat in the Middle East (CENTO), and Soviet and/or Chinese one in the Far East (SEATO). The USA, UK, France, Australia, New Zealand, Philippines, Thailand and Pakistan created CENTO in 1954 (The Manila Treaty). SEATO was created in 1959 by Britain, Iran, Turkey and Pakistan, with the support, but not full membership, of the US.

2 Memorandum, FO, 19 September 1952, FO 371/101263 TNA

3 Lowe, *Contending with Nationalism and Communism*, p. 75.